Gluten-Free Bread

Date: 2/18/14

641.5638 BRO
Brown, Ellen,
Gluten-free bread : more than
100 artisan loaves for a

PALM BEACH COUNTY
LIBRARY SYSTEM
3650 Summit Boulevard
West Palm Beach, FL 33406-4198

Gluten-Free Bread

More than 100 Artisan Loaves for a Healthier Life

ELLEN BROWN

RUNNING PRESS
PHILADELPHIA • LONDON

Copyright © 2013 by Ellen Brown
Photographs copyright © 2013 by Steve Legato

Published by Running Press,
A Member of the Perseus Books Group

All rights reserved under the Pan-American and International Copyright Conventions
Printed in China

This book may not be reproduced in whole or in part, in any form or by any means, electronic or mechanical, including photocopying, recording, or by any information storage and retrieval system now known or hereafter invented, without written permission from the publisher.

Books published by Running Press are available at special discounts for bulk purchases in the United States by corporations, institutions, and other organizations. For more information, please contact the Special Markets Department at the Perseus Books Group, 2300 Chestnut Street, Suite 200, Philadelphia, PA 19103, or call (800) 810-4145, ext. 5000, or e-mail special.markets@perseusbooks.com.

ISBN 978-0-7624-5005-3
Library of Congress Control Number: 2013933226
E-book ISBN 978-0-7624-5072-5

9 8 7 6 5 4 3 2 1
Digit on the right indicates the number of this printing

Cover and interior design by Jason Kayser
Edited by Kristen Green Wiewora
Typography: Freight

Running Press Book Publishers
2300 Chestnut Street
Philadelphia, PA 19103-4371

Visit us on the web!
www.offthemenublog.com

It's seeing my family grow that raises my spirits
higher than a bowl of yeast dough. This book
is dedicated to Charlie Rose Cerami, the totally adorable
and enchanting addition to my wonderful
group of great-nephews and nieces, who bring so
much joy to my life.

CONTENTS

Acknowledgments

WHILE DEVISING RECIPES AND WRITING ARE SOLITARY—AND SOMETIMES lonely—activities, it takes the proverbial village to really bring a cookbook to fruition. My thanks go:

To Kristen Green Wiewora, who is a totally awesome editor, and whose vision for this book placed me on the right path.

To Jason Kayser, the inspired designer who created the visual subtlety of the book, and whose design makes it a delight to hold and read.

To Steve Legato, whose talent and versatility as a food photographer never ceases to amaze me, and who shares my taste in jazz.

To Carrie Purcell and Micah Morgan, the meticulous food stylists who accepted the challenge that baking gluten-free breads is not easy, and made each and every one of them look beautiful.

To Mariellen Melker, a wonderful prop stylist who captures the unique nature of every book.

To Annie Lenth, for handling the production process so seamlessly, and to Iris Bass for her eagle-eyed copyediting.

To Ed Claflin, my agent, for his constant support, encouragement, and humor.

To my dear family for their love and support, especially to Nancy and Walter Dubler; Ariela Dubler; Jesse Furman; Ilan, Mira, and Lev Dubler-Furman; Joshua Dubler; Lisa Cerami; Zahir Cerami; David Krimm; and Peter Bradley.

To my many friends who critiqued my work and gave me the thumbs-up that these breads passed the standard of "as good as if not better than" breads made with wheat flour. They include Christine Chronis, Edye DeMarco, Constance Brown, Kenn Speiser, Fox Wetle, Richard Besdine, Vicki Veh, Joe Chazan, Kim Montour, Nick Brown, Karen Davidson, and Bruce Tillinghast.

And to Patches and Rufous, my adorable feline housemates, who kept me company from their perches in the office and curled up on top of the stove to enjoy its warmth while I baked breads.

Preface

• • •

BREAD IS THE STAFF OF LIFE. IT IS *THE* ESSENTIAL FOOD. THE FIRST PETITION in the Lord's Prayer is "Give us this day our daily bread." It's not "Give us this day our daily banana smoothie."

Bread is our "go-to" food for all times of day. We have toast for breakfast and a sandwich for lunch. When you enter a restaurant, the waiter places a basket of bread on the table, and part of every formal china setting is a small plate known as the bread and butter dish.

We even value bread when it's past its prime. Stale loaves are given a second life as crispy croutons on salads, or soaked with eggs and milk to become French toast at breakfast or bread pudding for dessert.

And relative to other categories of food, breads are easy to make, especially if they're made with wheat flour. Those recipes are generally fairly short and contain few ingredients. But to replace that wheat flour—just one line in that short ingredient list—with gluten-free alternatives can balloon the number of ingredients to include six or seven different flours, all of which need to be individually measured. What was a simple process has become far more complex.

The plastic tub in which I store my gluten-free arsenal of dry goods is almost three feet long; it takes up about half of my dining room table, which seats six people comfortably when set for a meal—just to give you an idea of the number of "basics" you'll need to embrace for great gluten-free breads.

The reason for such an extensive pantry is that baking in general and gluten-free baking in particular are much more about precision and chemistry than they are about the spontaneity and wizardry that can be brought to a sauté or soup. Each of the myriad flours ground from gluten-free grains or beans and the starches made from vegetables or roots has its own properties. The proportion of each of these elements in a recipe can change the results of the final product, and I'm always after the ultimate flavor and texture in my breads.

That's why it is impossible to create one master formulation for a gluten-free equivalent of all-purpose flour. Increasing numbers of manufacturers want you to believe there is a "magic bullet" substance that only this manufacturer has in its product to replace wheat flour. But this approach will not give you delicious and nutritious gluten-free bread that I can show you how to create.

Each recipe in this book contains a balance of protein-rich flours and starches, as Chapter 1 explains in the detailed discussion of options. For example, teff flour has a naturally inherent sweetness, so it works harmoniously with the nuttiness of brown rice flour to give you delicious bread that does not crumble when you make it into a sandwich. But the proportion of one ingredient to another changes with each list of ancillary ingredients.

This is the fourth cookbook I've written dedicated to delicious foods made without wheat yet still full of flavor. My goal has always been to create recipes that are equivalent, if not superior, in both taste and texture to those made with wheat flour. No one eating my recipes should ever say, "Not bad for gluten-free."

That is a high bar to set, and I hope that after you've prepared the recipes in this book, you'll agree that I meet it. I want everyone following a gluten-free diet to enjoy one of life's great foods—be it a slice of dense and chewy whole-grain bread dotted with healthful seeds, a feathery light and buttery slice of toasted brioche, a bagel layered with cream cheese and smoked salmon, a tender buttermilk biscuit to sop up the gravy on fried chicken, or vibrant cornbread laced with smoky bacon and flavorful Cheddar.

It is increasingly clear that the scientific community is just now beginning to realize the number of medical conditions that can be helped by the change to a gluten-free diet. While celiac disease, an autoimmune disorder, has been known for decades to respond positively to a gluten-free diet, the connection between removing gluten—a naturally occurring substance that can be potentially harmful to millions—from the diet may be important for many other people seeking to lead healthy and active lives. Plus, the replacements for wheat flour have the added benefit of being far more nutritious than wheat.

I fully appreciate how difficult it is to abandon flour and have to snoop out all the ways it can be hidden in foods. People following a gluten-free diet need to read the ingredient labels for all of their supermarket purchases: While the presence of wheat flour in baked goods or boxes of dried pasta is obvious, millions of other products use either wheat flour or one of its derivatives as a thickener or stabilizer. For example, not even baking powder is exempt from scrutiny because while most brands use cornstarch as a minor ingredient, others use flour.

If you bake the breads in this book you have no fear about gluten and you're taking a bite leading to a healthier and happier you.

Happy baking!

Ellen Brown

Providence, Rhode Island

Introduction

• • •

THERE'S NOTHING INHERENTLY "BAD" ABOUT GLUTEN. IT'S NOT AN EVIL chemical produced in a test tube by a mad scientist, nor is it adding plaque to our coronary arteries. It shouldn't be grouped with trans fats or MSG. Gluten is what's formed when two of the thirty proteins found in wheat, rye, and barley get wet. That's all there is to it.

But what's evil is that this natural reaction can be harmful to the health of millions. Understanding the need to live gluten-free starts with understanding how gluten can cause life-threatening problems if not removed from the diet of those who cannot tolerate it. But the good news is that following a gluten-free diet can mitigate debilitating symptoms and pain in as little as a few months, and a change of diet is the only answer. The need is for food rather than a pharmacy.

Our bodies contain a complex and interlocking system to prevent harm: It contains a network of organs, glands, and cell types dedicated to warding off illness, which are all lumped under the heading of the immune system.

But sometimes the immune system has been mysteriously programmed incorrectly and attacks healthy cells rather than potentially harmful ones. These maladies are termed autoimmune diseases.

Autoimmune disorders are not fully understood; however, many medical authorities now accept some causes. The sources of these disorders include viruses, which change the information carried inside the cells; sunlight and other forms of radiation;

and certain chemicals and drugs. There is also believed to be a connection to sex hormones; many more women suffer from these disorders than do men.

There are more than eighty types of autoimmune disease, and they include lupus, rheumatoid arthritis, and Graves' disease; some medical authorities also believe that multiple sclerosis is caused by an autoimmune response. While the aggravating factors in many of these diseases is complex, in the case of celiac disease it is really rather easy. Celiac disease is caused by an autoimmune response to gluten.

All humans are unable to properly digest the gluten protein, not just people who suffer from celiac. Normal protein digestion involves a complete breakdown of protein into small particles called amino acids that are in turn absorbed by the small intestine and used by the body as a nutritional source. However, the vast majority of us without gluten intolerance don't appear to be affected negatively by the inability to properly digest gluten. The gluten merely passes through our digestive systems without being absorbed. Think of the gluten as small bits of Styrofoam; you don't gain any nutrition from them but they don't inflict harm.

But for those who are intolerant, the undigested gluten protein gets absorbed into the lining of the small intestine but is not seen by the body as a source of nutrition. To the contrary, the body's immune systems attack these protein particles as something that needs to be destroyed, in very much the same way as it would attack an invading organism such as a virus, bacterium, or parasite.

The attack by the immune system causes inflammation and damage to the small intestine, which prevents it from absorbing the nutrients from food that are important for staying healthy.

Normally, the small intestine is lined with tiny, hairlike projections called villi that resemble a shag carpet, but on a microscopic scale. It is these villi that work to absorb vitamins, minerals, and other nutrients from the food we eat. When those villi are damaged by gluten, the inner surface of the small intestine becomes less like a plush carpet and more like a tile floor. The body is unable to absorb nutrients and the result is malnutrition.

It is now clear that the disease—which was thought to be most prevalent in people of Northern European ancestry but now is also found in Hispanic, African American, and Asian populations—is far more common than doctors once believed and is still underdiagnosed. Up until ten years ago, medical schools taught that celiac disease was relatively rare and only affected about 1 in 2,500 people. It was also thought to be a disease that primarily affected children and young people. But it is far greater. One federal study estimates that 1 in every 133 Americans suffers from it; that's more than 3 million people, which is four times more common than it was fifty years ago.

Dr. Joseph Murray, a gastroenterologist at the Mayo Clinic, compared blood samples taken in the 1950s with those taken from Americans today. It confirmed that celiac disease is actually increasing. One reason for that might be the changes in the actual wheat milled into today's flour.

In the 1950s, scientists began crossbreeding strains of wheat to make it heartier and shorter; this was part of the Green Revolution that boosted harvests worldwide and won Norman Borlaug, an American plant scientist, the Nobel Peace Prize in 1970 for his work with wheat. But Dr. Murray believes that this "new and improved" wheat might be a culprit in the rise of celiac disease.

This attitude forms the basis of the current theory popularized by best-selling author and cardiologist Dr. William Davis in his book *Wheat Belly: Lose the Wheat, Lose the Weight and Find Your Path Back to Health.* Dr. Davis believes that modern wheat can be classified as an opiate, due to its gliadin content. "This thing [the gliadin protein] binds into the opiate receptors in your brain and in most people it stimulates appetite, such that we consume four hundred and forty more calories per day, three hundred and sixty-five days a year," said Dr. Davis during a recent interview on *CBS This Morning.* Americans, therefore, are "wheat addicts," which adds to their weight while not adding much in the way of nutrients.

By contrast, gluten-free grains such as buckwheat, quinoa, millet, and sorghum are packed with nutrients not found in wheat flour, yet these grains are underutilized in most Americans' diet. Dr. Davis estimates that millions of people not suffering from celiac or any disease possibly tied to gluten are adopting a gluten-free diet because its nutritional profile is superior to wheat's.

Many of these bread recipes call for ground chia seeds as an ingredient, to help create dough that stays together. This ancient food, the basis for the Aztec and Mayan diets, is now being touted as a fantastic source of nutrition, while wheat flour contains few properties that enhance general health.

But the sad part is that many people suffering from celiac disease are unaware of the cause of their problems. It is estimated that 85 percent of Americans who have celiac disease are undiagnosed or misdiagnosed with other conditions. Dr. Daniel Leffler from the Celiac Center at Beth Israel Deaconess Medical Center in Boston believes that it takes an average of six to ten years for the average person with celiac disease to be properly diagnosed, even though the test for it is rather straightforward.

The condition is diagnosed by testing the blood for three antibodies—antigliadin, antiendomysial, and antitissue transglutaminase—all of which are present when an affected person is exposed to gluten, but which disappear when the offending grains are no longer consumed.

Millions more people whose digestive problems don't fall under the strict definition of celiac disease because they do not test positively for these antibodies have found that following a gluten-free diet helps them. Termed gluten-sensitive, rather than gluten-intolerant, this group could include up to 30 percent of the American population.

For this much larger group, eliminating gluten can eliminate symptoms ranging from migraines to abdominal pain to osteoporosis to sinus congestion. Gluten sensitivity has also been linked to such conditions as psoriasis, anemia, and asthma. A few researchers even suggest that a gluten-free diet helps control some of the symptoms of autism. A breakthrough study published in 2002 in the *New England Journal of Medicine* listed fifty-five diseases tied to gluten.

Following a gluten-free diet is not temporary, like cutting calories to lose five pounds after the holidays. It's for life. Eliminating gluten doesn't cause the body to become less sensitive to it. The condition for which the gluten was eliminated can return as soon as gluten is reintroduced to the diet.

But following a gluten-free diet is easier today than ever before. According to a study released in 2009, the market for gluten-free products grew at a compound annual growth rate of 28 percent from 2004 to 2008, capturing almost $2.6 billion in retail sales during 2010, and is anticipated to rise to $5 billion by 2015.

A large percentage of this market, however, is for processed foods, and those foods carry the same negative connotations as do processed foods made with gluten. But it's possible to make delicious homemade foods using gluten-free ingredients. And a good place to start is by baking breads.

CHAPTER 1

The Gluten-Free Pantry and Bread Basics

It's not easy to follow a gluten-free diet. Wheat flour and contaminated ingredients are all around you. But in reality it's far easier to follow the regimen when you're cooking for yourself at home, rather than trusting that restaurants really know what's in their food. Plus, when baking bread at home, you have the added benefit of an anticipatory aroma: There's nothing like that fresh-baked smell of bread wafting out of the oven to trigger your taste buds.

The movement into which these breads can be placed is artisanal foods. These are handcrafted loaves with character and flavor. They fall into the category of "everything old is new again." Until the development of large-scale commercial baking in the late-nineteenth century, all bread could have been deemed artisan. They were mixed and shaped by hand and baked by a professional baker or cook. They had holes that were not uniformly spaced, and they had a thick, chewy crust. You knew you were eating bread, not soft and fluffy air.

But then came a new standard in the 1920s, when snowy white Wonder Bread was introduced, and the gold standard of excellence became soft and sweet bread that was as light as the perky balloons on the wrapper. Packaged presliced bread that fit perfectly into the slats of a toaster became the American norm.

The revival of interest in eating coarse-grained handmade loaves of bread started in the 1980s, when baking bread at home was a hallmark of the whole new interest in food connoisseurship.

Bakeries similar to those in Europe began to pop up in major North American cities, especially in Northern California. Many of these bakeries were also selling coffee beans from around the world, and European cheeses. The appeal of their breads was a dense texture conveyed in a less-than-perfect-looking loaf.

The home cook could relate to these loaves, and bread baking became a weekend pastime for the self-proclaimed gourmet set. While whole grains were then integrated with wheat flour to produce those breads, today's gluten-free breads replace the flour with grains and starches ground from all sorts of vegetal sources.

In this chapter you'll be introduced to the myriad elements from which you can make delicious breads, ones that you know are gluten-free and created from your own high-quality ingredients.

THE ROLE OF GLUTEN IN TRADITIONAL BAKING

The first step in gluten-free bread baking is to understand the role that gluten plays in traditional breads. Most breads depend on gluten to succeed; gluten is a versatile protein that, when developed, forms a strong air-trapping network that creates breads' characteristic honeycomb structure and crumb.

In gluten-free breads, the goal is no different. But it is more complicated to re-create wheat breads' thick crusts and inside soft airy pockets without what many would consider a very essential component to what makes bread, well, bread.

While eliminating rye and barley from the gluten-free diet presents some challenges, eliminating all forms of wheat and wheat flour is a Herculean task—especially when baking bread. Wheat flour contains as many as thirty proteins, and two of those—glutenin and gliadin—form gluten when moistened with any liquid ingredient. These two proteins grab water and connect to form elastic strands of gluten. If flour has a lot of these proteins, it grabs up water faster, making the strong and springy gluten that is needed to bake bread; that's why high-protein bread flour is frequently specified in recipes for wheat breads. The formation of this elastic gluten network serves many functions in a bread dough. Like a net, gluten traps and holds air bubbles created by the natural leavening of yeast or the chemical leavening of baking soda or baking powder. When a dough is baked, the stretched flour proteins become rigid as moisture evaporates from the heat of the oven, and sets the breads' structure.

Replicating this structure is no easy task. There is no magic wand that can remove the gluten from wheat flour, because the proteins are built into the DNA of the wheat plant. But with the addition of a few other ingredients to nonwheat flours, the results can be just as good.

LOOKING FOR GLUTEN

Reading labels is essential to following a gluten-free diet, and it's not just for wheat, it's for rye and barley, too. Most products that contain gluten from common wheat are now labeled, due to the Food Allergen Labeling and Consumer Protection Act of 2006. But there are other ways wheat can be listed. Kamut, spelt, and farro are ancient types of wheat, and bulgur is cracked wheat kernels. Also be on the lookout for couscous, which, contrary to popular belief, is a granular pasta made with wheat flour and not a grain. Other forms of wheat include triticale, semolina, farina, and durum. If you see a product with one of these terms, it contains gluten. Be wary of oats if they are not certified as gluten-free. That's the only protection that they were not grown with wheat or processed with wheat. Gluten is also found in many processed foods. Caramel color, modified food starch, hydrolyzed vegetable protein, dextrin, and imitation seafood may contain gluten. It may be added as fillers to spices and various meats, such as hamburgers and hot dogs. Possible other additives with gluten include foreign-manufactured citric acid, blue cheese, diglycerides, gum base, malt, maltodextrin, and monogylcerides.

A GUIDE TO GLUTEN-FREE FLOURS AND STARCHES

Unfortunately, there is no single ingredient with which you can make a one-to-one substitution for all-purpose wheat flour when making gluten-free breads. But while these recipes might appear long, the ingredients are readily available.

If you visit the gluten-free baking aisle of supermarkets or the virtual aisles on the web, you'll discover a dizzying array of products that can be used to replace wheat flour;

and, in addition to being free of gluten, many of them are far more nutritious than wheat flour, too. Unbleached all-purpose flour contains very little protein when compared with the content of garbanzo bean flour or millet flour, and increasing the nutritional content is the reason why some people are turning to a gluten-free diet.

Each substance in the gluten-free arsenal has different properties. One will strengthen, another will act as a tenderizer, and another will add moisture. Wheat has all of these properties, which explains why multiple flours are needed to stand in for just one.

There are two basic categories of ingredients:

- Protein/fiber flours, such as brown rice flour, millet flour, garbanzo bean flour, and sorghum flour, provide structure, stability, flavor, color, texture, and nutrition.

- Starches, such as cornstarch, tapioca flour, potato starch, and sweet rice flour, are very fine in texture and create breads that have a soft crumb and a smooth texture.

You need a mix of the two categories to succeed. If you use only protein- and fiber-packed flours, your breads end up heavy and very dense. I had a few loaves of bread emerge from my oven that could easily have been used as doorstops. On the other hand, starches alone cannot provide enough structure for breads to hold their shape, and you'd end up with a pile of crumbs. Successful gluten-free baking begins with using the right flour blend—both protein/fiber flours and starches together—to get good results. The right combination can produce excellent results, often indistinguishable from breads made with wheat. Think of gluten-free bread baking as Goldilocks trying out beds: One is too hard, one is too soft, and the last is just right.

The ingredients listed here are the ones I've made use of in this book. There are many other options out there, but I tried to streamline the list to keep the expenses down; all of the baking aids here work overtime in multiple recipes.

Almond meal: Almond meal is a dream in gluten-free recipes. It adds protein, fiber, and essential minerals to recipes, not to mention a delicious almond taste. Of all the nut flours, this is the only one that is consistently available prepackaged because it has been used for so many desserts, such as classic French *macarons,* for centuries. You can grind blanched almonds in a spice grinder or food processor to make your own. You can also substitute such nuts as peeled hazelnuts or pecans for the almonds. Other nuts don't work as well; walnuts can be oily and pine nuts don't have enough flavor.

Buckwheat flour: Buckwheat flour, one of my favorites along with millet flour, is high in protein and fiber and has a lovely nutty taste. Contrary to popular belief, buckwheat is not related to wheat, nor is it a cereal grain: it's actually a fruit seed in the rhubarb family, which also includes sorrel. Buckwheat is high in manganese, an essential trace mineral.

Cornmeal: We are all familiar with cornmeal, and it is important to buy it from a manufacturer that processes it in a facility not contaminated with gluten. Cornmeal is made by grinding dried corn kernels; the meal can be fine, medium, or coarse. Water-ground or stone-ground types are more nutritious than steel-ground because more of the corn kernel is retained. It's important to follow the recipe's recommendation for the grind of cornmeal because using a coarser grain can result in a gritty dish.

Cornstarch: Cornstarch is what is most often used to thicken gluten-free foods as well as in baking. Called corn flour in some countries, it should never be confused with cornmeal. Cornstarch is made by grinding the endosperm (inner tissue) of the corn kernel after the kernels have been steeped for a few days, which makes it possible to separate the outer germ from the endosperm. This very light powder can form lumps if added to a dish or dough by itself. That's why it's mixed with the other gluten-free dry ingredients for breads and always mixed with a small amount of cold water before it's added to hot liquid as a thickener.

Garbanzo bean flour: Almost any dried legume can be ground into flour, and my favorite is garbanzo bean flour because, like the legume from which it's ground, it has a mild, sweet,

and almost nutlike flavor. Bean flours in general and garbanzo bean flour in particular also have a really good nutritional profile. A quarter-cup of garbanzo bean flour contains 6 grams of protein and an impressive 10 percent of the recommended daily intake of iron.

Millet: You've seen millet many times without knowing it, if you maintain a bird feeder: It's one of the primary components of birdseed. Millet is a member of the grass family that is very high in protein and B vitamins, as well as being a good source of magnesium. Magnesium has been shown in studies to reduce the severity of asthma and the frequency of migraine attacks. Magnesium has also been shown to lower high blood pressure and reduce the risk of heart attack. Millet flour adds a slightly sweet taste to breads and is very easy to digest.

Potato starch: Potato starch is very different from potato flour, so be careful when you shop for it. Potato starch is made from raw potatoes, while potato flour is made from cooked potatoes. The flour is far denser, and the two cannot be substituted for each other. Like the potatoes from which it's made, potato starch is a good source of potassium.

Rice flour: This neutral-flavored flour is one of the most common substitutes for all-purpose wheat flour. Both white and brown rice can be made into flour, but the outer husk is always removed before grinding. Brown rice flour has a better nutritional profile because it does contain some fiber, and white rice flour tends to make breads gritty. I only use white rice flour when the end result is to be a very pale bread.

Sorghum flour: Sorghum is a cereal grain that originated about five thousand years ago in Africa, where it continues to be an important food source. It's sometimes called *milo* and in India it is known as *jowar*. Sorghum contains three times the natural fiber and twice the protein as white rice flour.

Soy flour: Soy flour is a high-protein flour ground from roasted soybeans. I use the defatted version that has had the oils removed; it is less prone to rancidity and I prefer to use butter as the fat in my dough. Soy flour has a distinctive yellow color, which adds visual richness to breads.

Sweet rice flour: Called *mochiko* in Japanese, it can be found in Asian markets as well as supermarkets, and while called "sweet" there is no sweetener added. It's made from glutinous short-grained Japanese rice, and it is similar to the starches because it adds body to dough.

Tapioca flour: Also called cassava flour, tapioca is derived from the yucca plant, which is a starchy tropical tuber. It adds body to breads as well as a chewy texture, and it helps breads to brown.

Teff flour: Teff is the staple grain of Ethiopia, and it's packed with protein, calcium, and iron. It's nutritionally rich because most of the grain is made up of bran and germ, which is ground into a flour, bringing with it all of teff's inherent nutrients. It takes 150 teff grains to equal the weight of a single wheat grain. Teff creates a deeply colored flour that is wonderful to use in dense and hearty peasant breads. Its flavor is slightly sweet and reminiscent of molasses.

WHAT ABOUT OATS?

Including oats as part of gluten-free diets has been controversial, but recent research has spurred many organizations to give oats the thumbs-up. Although oats do not contain gluten, it is possible to contaminate them with gluten-containing grains grown or processed nearby. The only oats recommended by a majority of celiac organizations in North America are those labeled "certified gluten-free" or "noncontaminated" on the package.

Purchasing and Storing Gluten-Free Flours

Unlike all-purpose wheat flour that can be stored in an airtight container at room temperature for many months, most of the protein/fiber flours used in gluten-free baking should be refrigerated once they have been opened. These include brown rice flour, millet flour, soy flour, and sorghum flour. If any of these flours are included in a flour blend, then the whole batch should be refrigerated. But do measure out the amounts needed for a recipe and allow them to reach room temperature before baking with these flours.

When you open a bag of one of the protein/fiber flours, it should have a pleasant grainy or nutty smell. Millet flour is very prone to rancidity, so do smell it carefully.

The starch flours—cornstarch, potato starch, and tapioca flour—should have no scent, and they can be stored at room temperature for up to a year.

ESSENTIAL BINDERS

Gluten gives dough strength, so that the air incorporated by yeast or chemical leavening agents is trapped until the heat of the oven cooks the proteins and forms a structure. Wheat breads would end up a pile of crumbs if not for their gluten. For gluten-free baking, there are other options—natural gums and other binders—that give gluten-free flours and starches that all-important "stretch factor," and also the inherent stickiness that we recognize as being breadlike.

Xanthan gum: You'll see that most of the recipes in this book contain a small amount of xanthan (pronounced *ZAHN-thun*) gum. It is mixed with the dry ingredients and then added along with them to the wet ingredients.

Sometimes called corn sugar gum, xanthan gum is a natural carbohydrate, not a food additive. It's produced by the fermentation of the bacteria *Xanthomonas campestris.* When this bacterium is combined with corn sugar, it creates a colorless translucent substance, which is then dehydrated and ground into xanthan gum.

You've already eaten xanthan gum many times; for example, manufacturers add xanthan gum to candy to prevent sugar crystals from forming and to many ice creams to give them a smooth texture and mouthfeel.

WHAT ABOUT GUAR GUM?

Guar gum is an alternative to xanthan gum and is sometimes called for in gluten-free recipes. I believe that xanthan gum is better in baked goods, while guar gum is excellent in cold foods, such as ice creams; that's why I don't use guar gum in this book. Guar gum is ground from seeds from a plant that grows primarily in areas of Pakistan and the northern parts of India.

Chia seeds: This ancient seed that sustained the Aztec and Mayan peoples is the most powerful vegetal source of essential omega-3 fatty acids. It has about three to ten times the oil content of other grains and is so rich in antioxidants that the seeds can be stored for a long period of time without becoming rancid. It is also an excellent source of calcium and the mineral boron, which acts as a catalyst for the body's absorption of calcium. Chia has a nutlike flavor, and it holds about nine times its weight in water, and thus thickens and emulsifies bread dough. Chia seeds should always be ground and soaked before adding them to the dough. But they soak very nicely in the same bowl where you're proofing the yeast, and take the same amount of time.

Unflavored gelatin: Just as gelatin adds body to mousses and cold dishes, it serves well in baked breads, too. When it's mixed into gluten-free bread dough, it binds the cold dough and then holds it together and keeps it from crumbling when it's baked. There's no need to presoak it because it absorbs and softens while the dough rises and bakes. Gelatin is made of collagen, the protein that occurs naturally in bones and connective tissue, as well as in skin.

Agar powder: This is an alternative to gelatin because gelatin is made from animal tissue, so many vegetarians will not use it. They rely upon this flavorless seaweed derivative as a substitute, and the two are used in the same amount. Like gelatin, agar, whose name comes from the Malay word for "jelly," is full of protein (though incomplete), and as a member of the seaweed family it is also high in many nutrients like iron. You can use it anywhere in the book where gelatin is used, in equal amounts.

OTHER HELPFUL INGREDIENTS

While gluten-free bread baking presents some unique challenges because of the variety of dry ingredients that must be used, the other categories of ingredients are virtually identical to those used in conventional baking. What you will find is different is the ratio of liquid to dry. Here are ones you'll find in the majority of these bread recipes:

Eggs: Eggs contribute to the structure of bread, which is why most breads list them in the ingredient list. Without the protein supplied by gluten, the role of eggs becomes more crucial. In addition to providing protein, they also create the steam needed for starches to become firm. Egg yolk is also a rich source of emulsifying agents, fat and lecithin, which make it easier to incorporate air into the dough.

A TOTAL PACKAGE

Eggs are considered the gold standard for protein, because they provide all ten essential amino acids. Eggs contain more than a dozen vitamins and minerals, including choline, which is important for brain development and memory.

Sugar: Sugar adds sweetness, as well as contributes to the browning process that takes place when bread is cooked. The browning occurs when the sugar reacts with the protein in eggs and the dairy solids of butter during baking, and the higher the sugar content of a bread dough, the browner it will become once baked. Sugar also holds moisture, which keeps breads fresher longer.

WHITE GOLD

The granulated sugar we take for granted today as a staple was once so rare and expensive it was called white gold. Sugar cane, the first source of sugar, is a perennial grass that originated in Asia but is now grown in virtually every tropical and subtropical region of the world. It was only during the nineteenth century that refining beets for their sugar became commonplace.

Fats: Fat is responsible for providing lubrication and a luxurious mouthfeel. I am a devotee of baking with only unsalted butter. The milk fat in butter contributes tenderness and color and helps build the structure of bread. But most important, it releases its delicious flavor. The other fat found in these bread recipes is olive oil. It is an essential addition to the Focaccia (page 141) and other Mediterranean breads.

Chemical leavening agents: A leavening agent is anything that increases the volume in breads by creating carbon dioxide. The two chemical leavening agents used for the quick breads in Chapter 5 of this book are baking soda and baking powder. Both of these produce carbon dioxide when they are mixed with moisture. Baking soda, also called bicarbonate of soda, must be combined with an acidic ingredient, such as buttermilk, to create carbon dioxide, while baking powder is a combination of baking soda and cream of tartar, which is inherently acidic. Baking

1/4 tsp (1.25ml)

soda is twice as strong as baking powder, but the two can be substituted for each other. It is important to look at baking powder carefully, however. Some brands use a small percentage of wheat starch as the "moisture absorption agent." Most, however, use cornstarch or potato starch, including such leading brands as Rumford and Davis, but do check labels carefully.

QUICK BREADS OF YESTERYEAR

Chemical leavening is nothing new; Amelia Simmons used pearl ash in her book *American Cookery*, published in 1796. Because carbon dioxide is released at a faster rate through the acid-base reaction than through the fermentation process provided by living yeast, breads made with chemical leavening became known as quick breads more than a century ago.

Nonfat dried milk powder: In addition to augmenting the nutritional profile of the breads with a healthy dose of calcium, the powder is high in protein, which helps the breads rise and keeps them moist once baked.

PROTECTING GLUTEN-FREE INGREDIENTS FROM CONTAMINATION

If you're new to gluten-free baking, the whole concept of contamination is perhaps new to you as well. Setting up your kitchen so that foods containing gluten and gluten-free foods never meet can take time, but it is time well spent.

Here are some rules to follow to ensure that your gluten-free products are not inadvertently contaminated by wheat flour or any gluten-containing food:

- Thoroughly wash cabinets where gluten-free products will be stored, and make sure everyone who uses the kitchen is aware that these cabinets contain only gluten-free food. But unless the kitchen is to be free of all gluten-containing foods, it's still wise to place gluten-free ingredients in airtight containers before storing them.

- Clean all the kitchen surfaces thoroughly before starting to prepare gluten-free dishes, and then change the dishrag and dish towel for a fresh one. Don't use a sponge because it cannot be properly cleaned to make it free from gluten. The same is true for porous surfaces, such as wooden cutting boards. Have special ones for gluten-free ingredients.

- Have separate containers of butter or margarine for gluten-free cooking. Crumbs from someone's morning toast could have landed on a stick of butter at breakfast.

- Have separate containers of all other ingredients used for gluten-free cooking. Even though there is no gluten in granulated sugar or salt, molecules of wheat flour could have landed on them.

- Always place the gluten-free foods on the top shelf of the refrigerator to avoid risks of spills on them.

- Foil is a great way to avoid contamination. Use foil to keep foods separate when preparing, cooking, or storing.

- Use stickers of different colors when storing gluten-free foods to segregate them from other foods.

ESSENTIAL EQUIPMENT

There is very little need for specialized equipment to prepare the recipes in this book. Here is a list of the machines and gadgets I used on a regular basis while developing these breads:

Stand mixer: A powerful standard mixer that sits on the counter is the best friend you can have, and it's specified in every recipe. While handheld mixers are fine for small tasks, the stand mixer is what is best for baking. The paddle attachment makes the thickest substance look easy to blend.

Accurate kitchen scale: While volume measurements are given in all recipes, the way professional bakers work is to weigh all the dry ingredients. Depending on how a flour or starch is measured by volume, it can be up to 15 percent in error of its weight.

Food processor: A dedicated corner of my dishwasher is given over to this workhorse of the kitchen. The work bowl of food processors is made of plastic, which can harbor food particles once scratched, and some of these food particles may contain gluten. For very little money, you can purchase a second work bowl for your gluten-free recipes.

Also clean the base of the processor very thoroughly with a soapy cloth to ensure there are no traces of gluten on the surface.

Spice or coffee grinder: It's very difficult to find ground chia seeds, and with a grinder devoted to gluten-free ingredients it's also possible to create your own nut flours and oat flour.

Wire cooling racks: Dedicated gluten-free cooling racks are essential and there's really no substitute for them. The type of rack on top of a broiler pan is too solid, and there's nothing that makes baked goods lose their texture, especially those made with gluten-free ingredients, faster than placing them on an impervious surface.

Microplane grater: These resemble a flat kitchen spatula but with tiny holes in it. They're fabulous for grating citrus zest and fibrous foods, such as ginger, and you can also use them for Parmesan cheese and even garlic cloves for other recipes.

Rubber spatulas: Most of the bread recipes are baked in loaf pans, and the tops of the loaves need to be smoothed before rising. A rubber spatula dipped in water accomplishes this task easily.

Pastry brushes: To give your loaves a shiny crust, most of them are brushed with egg wash before baking. Although pastry brushes are expensive, paint brushes are cheap. Feel free to use a new 1½-inch/3.75 cm natural-bristle paintbrush as a dedicated pastry brush.

Loaf pans: Both the 8½ × 4½-inch/21.25 × 9.25 cm and 9 × 5-inch/23 × 11 cm pans are specified for these recipes, and I prefer dark metal pans because they create a crisper crust, which is a challenge with gluten-free breads. Glass pans conduct heat better than metal, and you should lower the oven temperature by 25°F (14°C) if using a glass pan. Glass also takes longer to cool down, so the waiting time for removing breads from them should be 10 minutes longer.

CALCULATING PAN SIZES

The volume of the smaller loaf pan is 6 cups/1.4 L and the volume of the larger size is 8 cups/1.9 L. If you are not using the pan specified in the recipe, use your calculator to determine the ingredient amount. To downsize a recipe from the larger to the smaller pan, multiply the ingredients by 0.75. To increase a recipe for the larger pan, multiply by 1.25. With eggs, which cannot be changed so conveniently, there are other solutions: To downsize to the smaller pan, beat the egg or eggs in a small cup and figure out what three-quarters of the volume should be; to increase to the larger pan, add an additional yolk.

Pizza stone: While most of these breads are baked in loaf pans because gluten-free bread dough is softer than dough made with wheat flour, there are some hand-formed loaves, and placing the baking sheet on a preheated pizza stone is the most successful way to bake them. An alternative is to preheat another baking sheet and stack the two on top of each other in the oven.

Silicone baking mats: I've had the same roll of parchment paper for two years since I invested in a trio of reusable mats. They stay in place on the baking sheet rather than sliding all around, and in addition to using them for baking breads (and cookies!) I use them for such dishes as barbecued chicken in place of heavy-duty aluminum foil. They are not inexpensive, but they are well worth it and you'll never have to grease a baking sheet again.

BAKING BASICS

What is included in this section isn't just for gluten-free breads. It's for all baking, regardless of whether the form is bread, pie, or cake, and whether the ingredient list includes wheat flour or a variety of gluten-free options.

Measure accurately. As noted earlier, all of these recipes give alternatives for measuring by volume or weight. If using volume, measure dry ingredients in plastic or metal dry measuring cups, which come in sizes of ¼, ⅓, ½, and 1 cup. Spoon dry ingredients from the container or canister into the measuring cup, and then sweep the top with a straight edge, such as the back of a knife or a spatula, to measure it properly. Do not dip the cup into the canister or tap it on the counter to produce a level surface. These methods pack down the dry ingredients, and can increase the actual volume by up to 15 percent. Measuring spoons are likewise a volume tool, and if the box or can does not have a straight edge built in, level the excess in the spoon back into the container with the back of a knife blade.

Measure liquids in transparent glass or plastic liquid measures. To accurately measure liquids, place the measuring cup on a flat counter and bend down to read the marked level.

Have all ingredients at room temperature. Almost all gluten-free breads are made with eggs because of their function in creating structure, and adding cold eggs to a yeast bread dough can be disastrous. Yeast needs a warm environment in which to rise properly. That's why the yeast is proofed with warm liquid. All the other ingredients should be at room temperature.

Just as you don't want cold ingredients to retard the yeast, if an ingredient is too hot it can kill the yeast. That's why butter is cooled after it's melted.

Preheat the oven properly. Some ovens can take up to 25 minutes to reach a high temperature, such as 450°F/230°C. The minimum heating time devoted to preheating the oven, even to a moderate temperature, such as 350°F/175°C, should be 15 minutes.

3½
CUPS
24oz
2½
20oz
16oz
12oz

Read the recipe thoroughly. This means that you have accounted in advance for all ingredients required for a recipe, so you don't get to a step and realize you must improvise. The French call this advance preparation of ingredients *mise en place*.

THE MAGIC OF YEAST

Yeast is a single-celled fungus, of which hundreds of species have been identified. Those of the genera *Saccharomyces* and *Candida* are the most useful for culinary purposes. The single cells are very small: Hundreds of millions of them would fit into a teaspoon. While green plants feed via photosynthesis, yeast feeds on carbohydrates and excretes alcohol, while producing carbon dioxide. That's why yeast is as good a friend of the brewer as it is of the baker. Given plenty of air and some food, yeast grows fast and produces a lot of carbon dioxide. It is the pressure of this gas that makes the bread rise. Only a little alcohol is formed. However, in a fermentation vat, where there is almost no air but an abundance of food in the form of sugar, the yeast cells change to a different mode, breathing little and concentrating on turning sugar into alcohol.

In addition to fermenting and flavoring other foods, yeasts themselves may also be used as food. They contain much protein and all but one of the B vitamins. They are consequently used to provide dietary supplements for countries whose citizens are on diets deficient in protein.

STEP-BY-STEP TO PERFECT YEAST BREAD

Here's the first rule for making delicious gluten-free bread: Forget everything you know about baking bread, and everything you know about how the dough should look. You're not going to be kneading the dough, because there's no gluten to develop! You won't end up with a ball of dough that is elastic and spongy to the touch and that springs back instantly if you poke it with your finger.

For gluten-free bread, you will use the paddle attachment of a stand mixer, rather than the dough hook. Even though I call them "doughs" because dough is what you create for breads, they are really more like batters in consistency. When handling gluten-free dough, keep in mind that it is delicate, and treat it accordingly. There are, however, some variations in texture.

Some of the doughs have the moderately thick consistency of the batter for a quick bread or layer cake; they are viscous but still pourable and you couldn't hold a handful because the batter would run through your fingers. These are the recipes that are allowed to rise in the loaf pan in which they'll be baked. The reason you bake them before they crown over the top of the pan is that the texture of the batter is so delicate that they might just spill over onto the counter or into the oven if allowed to rise higher. These doughs are not formed with your hands in any way, nor do they undergo a first rise in a mixing bowl.

However, some of the doughs have the consistency of a thick brownie batter, one that you would spread into a pan with a rubber scraper. Although they have to be handled gently, these bread doughs can be formed after an initial rise.

Then there are a few recipes that create dough with the consistency of a drop biscuit dough. These are closest to doughs made with wheat flour, but they are still delicate and must be treated gently at all times.

Proofing the yeast: Yeast is a living organism and you really need validation that it's alive and kicking before you add any other ingredients. To proof the yeast (as in "to prove that it's alive"), you need warm liquid and some ingredient to serve as food for the yeast. Most often, sugar fulfills that function. Until you learn to recognize what 110° to 115°F/43° to 46°C feels like on your wrist, use an instant-read thermometer to verify the temperature. Mix together the yeast, liquid, and food for the yeast, and let it sit aside for 10 minutes while you gather the rest of your ingredients. If it doesn't become foamy, it's dead. There's no reviving it. You can't give it CPR. The only option is to buy a new jar or package.

THE STORY OF YEAST

Commercially produced yeast first appeared in the United States in the 1860s. Charles and Maximillian Fleischmann, immigrants from Austria-Hungary who settled in Cincinnati, patented and sold standardized cakes of compressed yeast. By the early twentieth century, factory-produced yeast was widely available. Cookbook recipes began specifying that commercial yeast be added directly to bread dough in sufficient quantities to leaven it in less than two hours.

Gathering all the remaining ingredients: If your eggs are straight out of the refrigerator, place them in a bowl of hot tap water for at least 5 minutes to bring them to room temperature. This is key because yeast needs a warm environment in which to rise and cold eggs can cool it down. By the same token, yeast can be killed by too hot a temperature, which is why butter is melted and then cooled before adding it to the dough.

Mixing the dry ingredients: Gluten-free flours are so finely milled that they could potentially billow about like a blizzard, so use a really deep mixing bowl to whisk them and keep the whisk very low in the bowl. Whisking them well is especially important if there is xanthan gum in the recipe, because if it's not mixed in evenly, you end up with pockets in your bread that taste like a sponge.

Putting it all together: I like to minimize the number of bowls to wash when I bake. That's why the yeast in these recipes is proofed in the bowl of a stand mixer. The remaining wet ingredients are then added to the yeast mixture, and the dry ingredients are added last.

It is possible to use a high-quality handheld mixer to make gluten-free bread dough. But the motor is not as powerful as that of a stand mixer, so increase the beating time by 2 minutes.

Allowing the dough to rise: Here's the step in which the magic occurs. The yeast is permitted to do its thing and make bubbles of carbon dioxide. The goal is to have the bread double in bulk, and depending on the formulation of the bread and the temperature of the kitchen, this can take between 40 minutes and 2 hours. Some breads rise just once before they're baked, and others are given a preliminary rise in a mixing bowl and then in their final shape or in a loaf pan. There is no hard-and-fast rule about this, and the recipes in this book that specify a double rise is only used for recipes in which the bread dough has the consistency to hold together.

The double rise tends to make the crumb more pleasing after the bread is baked because there are no large air pockets. Deflating the dough after the first rise and then allowing it to rise again ensures a more uniform interior.

GETTING A RISE

The right temperature is necessary for dough to rise. There are some tricks to creating a warm enough temperature in a cold kitchen. Set a foil-covered electric heating pad on low and put the bread dough on the foil; put the bread dough in the dishwasher and set it for just the drying cycle; put the bread dough in your gas oven to benefit from the warmth from the pilot light; preheat your oven to 150°F/65.5°C and then turn off the heat just before putting the bread dough in the oven; or put the bread dough in any cold oven over a large pan of boiling-hot water.

Baking the bread: This is fairly straightforward, but keeping an eye on the bread is recommended. Gluten-free bread has a tendency to brown faster than do breads made with wheat flour. That's why many recipes suggest covering the bread loosely with aluminum foil when it is partially baked.

Certain breads create a more crispy crust if they are baked in a humid environment, which is why most commercial bakeries have ovens that automatically pump in steam during the baking cycle. That is why there is a step in those recipes for adding a pan of boiling water and spraying the sides of the oven.

Cooling the bread: The breads must remain in their loaf pans or on their baking sheets for the amount of time specified or they may literally fall apart in your hands. Without gluten, the network created in the hot oven needs time to firm up. Many times I was tempted to ignore this rule because the bread smelled so wonderful that I wanted to taste it immediately, and I was always sorry.

CRUST TRICKS

Unfortunately the crispy bottom and side crusts on bread baked in a loaf pan have a tendency to soften during the time the loaf sits in the pan after being removed from the oven. The cooling time is essential so that the bread doesn't fall apart, but if you want to create crispy crust anew, keep the oven on and bake the loaf on a cooling rack set over a baking sheet for 5 to 10 minutes after removing it from the pan.

MAKING AN ACTIVE SOURDOUGH STARTER

The big difference between sourdough bread and the "normal" bread you buy or bake is the source of the yeast. Most bakers today use cultivated yeast that comes in a jar. The jar contains live yeast fungi that are dormant because they have been dried, preserved, and ground into a powder. You add flour, water, sugar, and salt to the yeast to make a loaf of bread. The water reactivates the yeast fungi, which feed on the sugar and starch to make the bread rise.

Sourdough bread deals with yeast in a completely different way. Sourdough yeast fungi are actually kept alive constantly in a liquid medium called a starter or "mother dough." It's the starter that gives sourdough bread its distinctive flavor.

If you want to be totally authentic, the starter begins by capturing wild yeast floating through the air in your house or the wild yeast on foods, such as leaves of red cabbage, that are submerged in the flour and water mixture. The nonauthentic ways of starting a starter are with a few teaspoons of dry yeast or begging a cup of starter from a nice friend.

I think that everyone who wants to know what it's like to adopt a cat or a dog, let alone have a baby, should start by being forced to successfully maintain a sourdough starter made with wild yeast for at least two months. This may sound severe, but making bread with active sourdough starter is a real commitment. You need to care for it in a loving way by feeding it promptly and giving it just the temperature and climatic conditions it likes.

Starting the Starter

Using the previous analogy, we'll call this the conception process of the starter, and a bonus is that you get to eat mashed potatoes, too. There are almost as many theories on how to start a starter as there are particles of yeast in the air. This is one that has never failed me, made with wheat flour or gluten-free ingredients.

3 (8-ounce/227 g) russet potatoes, peeled and cubed
1 quart/950 ml filtered water, plus 1 cup/237 ml filtered water
2 teaspoons/10 g fine salt
2 tablespoons/30 ml honey
1¼ cups/198 g brown rice flour, plus more for later feedings, if desired
2 cups/240 g millet flour, plus more for later feedings, if desired
¾ cup/95 g sorghum flour, plus more for later feedings, if desired
¾ cup/90 g teff flour, plus more for later feedings, if desired

Combine the potatoes and the 1 quart/950 ml of water in a saucepan and bring to a boil over medium-high heat. Lower the heat to low and simmer the potatoes for 12 to 15 minutes, or until tender. Drain the potatoes, reserving all the water. Enjoy the potatoes some other way.

Place the water in a large ceramic or plastic bowl and add the salt, honey, 1¼ cups/198 g of the rice flour, 1 cup/120 g of the millet flour, ¾ cup/95 g of the sorghum flour, and ¾ cup/90 g of the teff flour. Whisk the mixture well until smooth. Place an upside-down basket or piece of cheesecloth over the top of the bowl, and place it in a warm, draft-free spot.

After 24 hours, pour off 1 cup/237 ml of the mixture, and add the 1 cup/237 ml of water and remaining 1 cup/120 g of millet flour. After a few days, the starter will become frothy from the yeast's multiplying. Feed the starter twice a day, each time removing

1 cup/237 ml of liquid and adding 1 cup/237 ml of water and 1 cup/120 g of one of the grains in the initial formulation; do not use one particular grain exclusively.

After 5 days, the starter should be truly fermented and it will develop a strong aroma that is reminiscent of both bread and beer. By the end of the week, the starter should be light yellow and have the consistency of pancake batter, and there should be a watery liquid on the top called hooch. You've now done it. Your starter is started.

Maintaining and Using the Starter

If you want to keep your starter on the counter, remember that it must be fed twice a day by throwing out 1 cup/237 ml of the mixture and replacing it with water and additional flours. Remember that the starter is a living thing. But most people refrigerate the starter at this point, and at the lower temperature the yeast slows down its reproduction and the starter only needs feeding every 4 or 5 days.

Just remember that every time you remove starter from the bowl, you need to replace it immediately with equal amounts of water and some combination of cereal grain flours. Do not feed the starter with cornstarch, tapioca flour, or potato starch because they don't supply the necessary protein that the yeast needs to thrive.

CAUTION: Never cover the starter on the counter with anything that is airtight. The yeast is giving off carbon dioxide and if the starter is in a tightly closed jar, the pressure can build up and the container might explode.

Substituting Active Sourdough Starter for Packaged Yeast

An active sourdough starter is one that has fed within the past 12 hours, and that is active enough that it was able to double in size after that feeding.

One cup/237 ml of active sourdough starter has about the same leavening capabilities as 2¼ teaspoons/7 g of yeast. But because the starter has both flour and water in it, subtract ½ cup/120 ml of water and ¾ cup/90 g of dry ingredients (each of the gluten-free flours and starches at the ratio that they are listed to total ¾ cup/90 g) for every 1 cup/237 ml of sourdough starter used in your recipe.

KEEPING GLUTEN-FREE BREADS FRESH

Another role played by gluten in conventional bread is to retain moisture after baking, and gluten-free bread starts to dry out the minute it comes out of the oven.

The best way to keep it moist and fresh is to refrigerate it, once cooled, tightly wrapped in plastic wrap. I've discovered that the trick to keeping brown sugar moist—a slice of apple in the bag—also works with gluten-free bread if the loaf is kept refrigerated in a storage container rather than tightly wrapped in plastic.

But you can also slice it, wrap the slices individually in plastic, and freeze them.

CHAPTER 2

Basic Loaves

Most breads made with wheat flour are fairly lean and basic. The ingredient list can be as short as flour, water, and yeast. For gluten-free breads, the ingredient list is always far longer, but many of the results can be similar.

We think of artisan bread as being less industrial and more handcrafted, and those are the breads you will find in this chapter. However, there are differences. Most artisanal wheat breads are free form and take their shape from the hands of the baker. That is not the case with gluten-free breads; the majority are baked in loaf pans because of the soft texture of the dough. Despite this difference, you'll still find that chewy, filling quality of a good basic bread in this chapter.

These breads are fairly lean because they don't contain a large amount of butter or olive oil. Most of them are chewy and dense, but at the end of the chapter are four essential breads for every cook's repertoire: French baguette, sourdough boule, ciabatta, and white toasting bread.

Millet Buckwheat Bread

THIS IS A TRULY HEAVENLY PEASANT BREAD that delivers nutritious millet and nutty buckwheat as both grains and flours. Then, everything from sesame seeds to rolled oats and sunflower seeds adds a chewy texture. This is a wonderful choice for a bread to accompany a thick, hearty soup as supper. It can also be used in a more elegant setting if you toast thin slices to support slices of smoked salmon with the traditional garnishes of sour cream or cream cheese, chopped capers, and chopped red onion.

MAKES 2 LOAVES

½ cup/100 g millet
½ cup/82 g buckwheat groats (kasha)
2¼ teaspoons/7 g active dry yeast
½ cup/118 ml plus 1 tablespoon/15 ml honey, divided
2 tablespoons/30 g ground chia seeds
1½ cups/355 ml water, heated to 110° to 115°F/43° to 46°C, divided
2 cups/240 g millet flour
¾ cup/96 g cornstarch
¾ cup/127.5 g potato starch
¾ cup/93.75 g tapioca flour
¾ cup/90 g buckwheat flour
½ cup/64 g coarse yellow cornmeal
1 teaspoon/9 g xanthan gum
1 teaspoon/6 g fine salt
¼ cup/32 g sesame seeds
½ cup/48 g gluten-free old-fashioned rolled oats
1 large egg, beaten lightly
¾ cup/93 g unsalted sunflower seeds

Bring 1½ cups/355 ml of water to a boil in a medium-size saucepan over high heat. Stir in the millet and buckwheat groats. Remove the pan from the heat and cover it. Allow the grains to soak for 10 minutes, or until needed.

(recipe continues)

Combine the yeast, 1 tablespoon/15 ml of the honey, the chia seeds, and ¾ cup/178 ml of the warm water in the bowl of a stand mixer fitted with the paddle attachment and mix well. Set aside for about 10 minutes while the yeast proofs.

Combine the millet flour, cornstarch, potato starch, tapioca flour, buckwheat flour, cornmeal, xanthan gum, and salt in a deep mixing bowl and whisk well. Drain the millet and buckwheat groats, shaking them vigorously in a colander.

When the yeast looks frothy add the remaining ¾ cup/178 ml of warm water and the remaining ½ cup/118 ml of the honey and mix well. Add the dry ingredients, drained grains, sesame seeds, and oats. Beat at medium speed until combined. Increase the speed to high and beat the dough for 3 to 5 minutes, or until the dough has the consistency of a thick cake batter that would require spreading in a cake pan; it is too thick to pour.

Lightly grease the inside of a large mixing bowl with vegetable oil or softened butter. Scrape the dough out of the mixer bowl and into the greased bowl, smoothing the top with moistened fingers or a rubber spatula dipped in water. Cover the bowl loosely with a sheet of oiled plastic wrap or a damp tea towel and place it in a warm, draft-free spot. Allow the dough to rise for 1 hour, or until it has doubled in bulk.

Line a baking sheet with parchment or a silicone baking mat. Place the oven racks in the middle and lowest positions. Place a second rimmed baking sheet on the lower rack and place a pizza stone on the upper rack. Preheat the oven to 375°F/190°C toward the end of the rising time, bring a kettle of water to a boil, and have a spray bottle of water handy.

Punch down the dough, divide it in half, and form each half into an oblong on the lined baking sheet. Brush the top of the loaves with the egg wash and pat the sunflower seeds on top.

(*recipe continues*)

Pour 1 cup/237 ml of the boiling water into the heated sheet pan and slide the baking sheet on top of the heated pizza stone. Spray the walls of the oven with the spray bottle, close the oven door and wait 30 seconds, then spray the oven walls again.

Bake the bread for 40 to 45 minutes, or until the bread is golden brown, sounds hollow and thumps when tapped, and has reached an internal temperature of 190°F/87°C on an instant-read thermometer. Remove the bread from the oven and allow it to cool for 30 minutes before slicing.

NOTE:

The bread is best the day it is baked, but it can be stored refrigerated, tightly covered with plastic wrap, for up to 2 days.

VARIATION:

- To make the bread vegan, substitute pure maple syrup for the honey, and substitute 1½ teaspoons/4 g of egg replacement powder (such as Ener-G) mixed with 2 tablespoons/30 ml of water, for the beaten egg.

Sunflower "seeds" is actually a misnomer. The small disks are the fruit of the sunflower. Sunflower seeds are an excellent source of vitamin E, the body's primary fat-soluble nutrient, which neutralizes free radicals that otherwise might damage cell membranes. It also plays an important role in the prevention of cardiovascular disease. Along with pistachio nuts, sunflower seeds have been proven to reduce cholesterol. They have a mild flavor and are related botanically to Jerusalem artichokes.

Multigrain Fennel Bread

THIS BREAD IS MEDIUM BROWN in tone and the different grains give it an almost nutty flavor that balances nicely with the licorice notes from the fennel seeds. I like thick slices of this bread toasted and used as a base for fish stews, such as bouillabaisse and cioppino. The combination of cornmeal with sorghum and teff flour create a loaf with a definitively chewy texture, and that's a big part of its appeal to me.

MAKES 1 LOAF

2¼ teaspoons/7 g active dry yeast
2 teaspoons/8 g granulated sugar
1¼ cups/296 ml whole milk, heated to 110° to 115°F/43° to 46°C, divided
⅔ cup/84.7 g sorghum flour
⅓ cup/40 g teff flour
¼ cup/32 g finely ground yellow gluten-free cornmeal
½ cup/64 g cornstarch
½ cup/62.5 g tapioca flour
1 teaspoon/2 g unflavored gelatin or agar powder
1 teaspoon/9 g xanthan gum
¾ teaspoon/4.5 g fine salt
2 large eggs, at room temperature
3 tablespoons/42 g unsalted butter, melted and cooled
3 tablespoons/45 ml light molasses
2 tablespoons/12 g fennel seeds, crushed
½ cup/24 g gluten-free old-fashioned rolled oats

Spray the inside of a 9 × 5-inch/23 × 11 cm loaf pan with vegetable oil spray.

Combine the yeast, sugar, and ½ cup/118 ml of the warm milk in the bowl of a stand mixer fitted with the paddle attachment and mix well. Set aside for about 10

(recipe continues)

minutes while the yeast proofs. Combine the sorghum flour, teff flour, cornmeal, cornstarch, tapioca flour, gelatin, xanthan gum, and salt in a deep mixing bowl and whisk well.

When the yeast looks frothy add the remaining ¾ cup/178 ml of warm milk and the eggs, melted butter, and molasses and mix well. Add the dry ingredients and beat at medium speed until combined. Increase the speed to high and beat the dough for 3 to 5 minutes, or until it has the consistency of a thick but still pourable cake batter. Beat in the fennel seeds.

Scrape the dough into the prepared pan, smooth the top with a rubber spatula dipped in water, and cover the pan with a sheet of oiled plastic wrap or a damp tea towel. Allow the bread to rise in a warm place for 40 to 50 minutes, or until it reaches ½ inch/1.25 cm from the top of the pan. Sprinkle the top of the loaf with the oats.

Preheat the oven to 350°F/175°C toward the end of the rising time.

Covering the loaf loosely with aluminum foil after 30 minutes, bake the bread for 50 to 55 minutes, or until the bread is golden brown, the top is firm, and it has reached an internal temperature of 190°F/87°C on an instant-read thermometer. Remove the bread from the oven and allow it to cool for 30 minutes. Remove it from the loaf pan by running a spatula around the rim and invert it onto a cooling rack to cool completely.

NOTE:

The bread is best the day it is baked, but it can be stored refrigerated, tightly covered with plastic wrap, for up to 2 days.

VARIATIONS:

- Substitute caraway seeds for the fennel seeds.
- Add ½ cup/72 g of dried currants or finely chopped dried apricots to the dough.

Dark Pumpernickel

TRADITIONAL PUMPERNICKEL is associated with the Westphalian region of Germany, and references to it date back to the mid-fifteenth century. The authentic version is made with rye flour and a sourdough starter, and the color results from a very long baking time. Of course, rye cannot be used in a gluten-free bread, but caraway seeds are added to replicate the flavor. In this loaf, the color is primarily due to the cocoa, espresso powder, and molasses in the dough, but the bread's primary flavor is a nice rich blend.

MAKES 1 LOAF

- 2 tablespoons/30 g ground chia seeds
- 2¼ teaspoons/7 g active dry yeast
- 2 tablespoons/27 g firmly packed light brown sugar
- 1 cup/237 ml water, heated to 110° to 115°F/43° to 46°C
- 2 cups/316 g brown rice flour, plus more if needed
- ⅔ cup/84.7 g sorghum flour
- ½ cup/62.5 g tapioca flour
- ½ cup/64 g cornstarch
- ½ cup/34 g nonfat dried milk powder
- ⅓ cup/40 g buckwheat flour
- 3 tablespoons/15 g unsweetened cocoa powder
- 1½ teaspoons/13.5 g xanthan gum
- 1 teaspoon/6 g fine salt
- 1 teaspoon/2 g instant espresso powder
- 3 large eggs, at room temperature
- ¼ cup/59 ml vegetable oil
- ¼ cup/59 ml light molasses
- 1 teaspoon/5 ml cider vinegar
- 1 tablespoon/7 g caraway seeds, crushed

Combine the chia seeds, yeast, brown sugar, and water in the bowl of a stand mixer fitted with the paddle attachment and mix well. Set aside for about 10 minutes

(recipe continues)

while the yeast proofs. Combine the 2 cups/316 g of rice flour and the sorghum flour, tapioca flour, cornstarch, milk powder, buckwheat flour, cocoa powder, xanthan gum, salt, and espresso powder in a deep mixing bowl and whisk well.

When the yeast looks frothy add the eggs, oil, molasses, and vinegar and mix well. Add the dry ingredients and caraway seeds and beat at medium speed until combined. Increase the speed to high and beat the dough for 3 to 5 minutes, or until the dough holds together and has the consistency of a drop biscuit dough. Add more rice flour by 1 tablespoon/10 g amounts to make the dough thicker, if necessary.

Lightly grease the inside of a large mixing bowl with vegetable oil or softened butter. Scrape the dough out of the mixer bowl into the greased bowl, smoothing the top with moistened fingers or a rubber spatula dipped in water. Cover the bowl loosely with a sheet of oiled plastic wrap or a damp tea towel and place it in a warm, draft-free spot. Allow the dough to rise for 1 hour, or until it has doubled in bulk.

Cover a baking sheet with parchment paper or a silicone baking mat. Punch down the dough. Form the dough into a 10-inch/25 cm round on the prepared baking sheet. Cover the loaf with a sheet of oiled plastic wrap and allow it to rise in a warm place for 45 to 50 minutes, or until doubled in size.

Place the oven racks in the middle and lowest positions. Place a second rimmed baking sheet on the lower rack and place a pizza stone on the upper rack. Preheat the oven to 375°F/190°C toward the end of the rising time, bring a kettle of water to a boil, and have a spray bottle of water handy.

Pour 1 cup/237 ml of the boiling water into the heated sheet pan and slide the lined baking sheet on top of the heated pizza stone. Spray the walls of the oven with the spray bottle, close the oven door and wait 30 seconds, then spray the oven walls again. Covering the loaf loosely with aluminum foil after 30 minutes, bake the

(*recipe continues*)

bread for 45 to 55 minutes, or until the bread is dark brown, sounds hollow and thumps, and has reached an internal temperature of 190°F/87°C on an instant-read thermometer. Remove the bread from the oven and allow it to cool for 30 minutes before slicing.

NOTE:

The bread is best the day it is baked, but it can be stored refrigerated, tightly covered with plastic wrap, for up to 2 days.

VARIATION:

- Omit the caraway seeds, increase the brown sugar to ¼ cup/55 g, and add ½ to ⅔ cup/72 to 97 g of raisins to the dough.

There are two types of cocoa on the market: natural and Dutch-process. Dutch-process cocoa powder has an extra step in the production process. Before the shelled beans are ground they are soaked in an alkaline solution to neutralize their natural acidity. This removes any bitter or sour flavors in the cocoa, and also turns it a darker color than natural cocoa powder. If a recipe does not specify a type of cocoa, know that Dutch-process cocoa will give whatever you're making a darker color and a more complex flavor, whereas natural cocoa powder tends to be fruitier-tasting and lighter in color.

HEARTY PUMPERNICKEL STUFFING

I've often thought we really do stuffing an injustice by serving it only in conjunction with holiday birds. I serve stuffing all year long, and with all sorts of protein. It's just another carbohydrate to me, like potatoes or rice. Here is my all-purpose stuffing recipe, and the Dark Pumpernickel makes it a heartier dish.

SERVES 4 TO 6

6 tablespoons (¾ stick)/83 g unsalted butter
1 large onion, diced
3 celery ribs, diced
1 cup/237 ml chicken stock
3 tablespoons/11 g chopped fresh parsley
2 tablespoons/4 g chopped fresh sage (substitute 1 teaspoon/0.7 g dried)
2 teaspoons/1.6 g fresh thyme leaves (substitute ½ teaspoon/0.5 g dried)
3 cups/135 g crumbled stale Dark Pumpernickel
Salt and freshly ground black pepper to taste

Heat the butter in a large, covered skillet over medium-high heat. Add the onion and celery and cook, stirring frequently, for 3 minutes, or until the onion is translucent. Add the stock, parsley, sage, and thyme and bring to a boil, stirring occasionally. Lower the heat to low, cover the skillet, and simmer the mixture for 15 minutes, or until the vegetables are tender. Stir in the bread and season to taste with salt and pepper.

Transfer the stuffing to the prepared pan. Cover the pan with aluminum foil and bake for 30 minutes. Remove the foil and bake for an additional 10 minutes, or until the top is slightly crisp.

(recipe continues)

VARIATIONS:

- Sauté ½ pound/227 g of bulk pork sausage over medium-high heat, breaking up lumps with a fork, for 5 to 7 minutes, or until browned. Remove the sausage from the pan with a slotted spoon and set aside. Reduce the butter to 4 tablespoons (½ stick)/56 g, increase the sage to 3 tablespoons/6 g, and omit the thyme. Return the sausage to the pan when adding the stock and herbs.
- Add ½ pound/228 g of cooked chopped chestnuts before baking the stuffing.
- Add ½ pound/228 g of mushrooms, wiped with a damp paper towel, trimmed, and chopped, to the skillet along with the onion and celery.
- Preheat the oven to 350°F/175°C and line a baking sheet with foil. Bake ½ cup/59 g of chopped walnuts for 5 to 7 minutes, or until lightly browned. Fold the walnuts into the stuffing just prior to baking.
- Substitute 1 small fennel bulb, chopped, for the celery, and add 1 teaspoon/2 g of crushed fennel seeds.

Muesli Bread

THERE ARE SO MANY healthful and flavorful ingredients in the muesli—including dried fruits and nuts—that this bread just sings with flavor and texture. I think of this bread as "breakfast on the go." If you don't have the time to sit down and eat a bowl of muesli, spread a toasted slice of this with cream cheese to gain some of the valuable nutrients in dairy. In addition to being a great breakfast bread, it works very well served with poultry and pork dishes at dinner. If there are any leftovers, turn it into a batch of bread pudding and extend the life of these healthy ingredients to dessert.

MAKES 1 LOAF

2 tablespoons/30 g ground chia seeds
2¼ teaspoons/7 g active dry yeast
2 tablespoons/25 g granulated sugar
1½ cups/355 ml water, heated to 110° to 115°F/43° to 46°C, divided
1½ cups/180 g gluten-free oat flour
½ cup/62.5 g tapioca flour
½ cup/85 g potato starch
¼ cup/17 g nonfat dried milk powder
1 teaspoon/2 g unflavored gelatin or agar powder
1½ teaspoons/13.5 g xanthan gum
½ teaspoon/3 g fine salt
2 large eggs, at room temperature
4 tablespoons (½ stick)/56 g unsalted butter, melted and cooled
1 cup/116 g gluten-free muesli cereal (such as Bob's Red Mill), divided

Spray the inside of an 9 × 5-inch/23 × 11 cm loaf pan with vegetable oil spray.

Combine the chia seeds, yeast, sugar, and ¾ cup/178 ml of the warm water in the bowl of a stand mixer fitted with the paddle attachment and mix well. Set aside for about 10 minutes while the yeast proofs. Combine the oat flour, tapioca flour,

(recipe continues)

potato starch, milk powder, gelatin, xanthan gum, and salt in a deep mixing bowl and whisk well.

When the yeast looks frothy add the remaining ¾ cup/178 ml of warm water and the eggs and melted butter and mix well. Add the dry ingredients and ¾ cup/87 g of the muesli and beat at medium speed until combined. Increase the speed to high and beat the dough for 3 to 5 minutes, or until it has the consistency of a thick but still pourable cake batter.

Scrape the dough into the prepared pan, smooth the top with a rubber spatula dipped in water, and cover the pan with a sheet of oiled plastic wrap or a damp tea towel. Allow the bread to rise in a warm place for 40 to 50 minutes, or until it reaches ½ inch/1.25 cm from the top of the pan. Sprinkle the top with the remaining ¼ cup/29 g of muesli.

Preheat the oven to 375°F/190°C toward the end of the rising time.

Covering the loaf loosely with aluminum foil after 30 minutes, bake the bread for 50 to 55 minutes, or until the bread is golden brown, the top is firm, and it has reached an internal temperature of 200°F/93°C on an instant-read thermometer. Remove the bread from the oven and allow it to cool for 30 minutes. Remove it from the loaf pan by running a spatula around the rim and invert it onto a cooling rack to cool completely.

NOTE:

The bread is best the day it is baked, but it can be stored refrigerated, tightly covered with plastic wrap, for up to 2 days.

MAKING YOUR OWN MUESLI

A Swiss doctor, Maximilian Bircher-Benner, first introduced muesli to the patients at his clinic in about 1900. Dr. Bircher-Benner was one of the first doctors to advocate eating a large amount of whole grains as part of a healthful diet. Due to the large percentage of oats in most formulations, it's wise to only purchase muesli that is certified as gluten-free. Packaged muesli is far more expensive to buy than any of its component ingredients, and it's very easy to make. Here is a short recipe:

MAKES 6 CUPS MUESLI

4 cups/384 g gluten-free old-fashioned rolled oats
½ cup/72 g chopped raw almonds
½ cup/54 g chopped pecans
½ cup/37 g sweetened or unsweetened shredded coconut
½ cup/80 g pumpkin seeds
1½ teaspoons/1.5 g ground cinnamon
¼ teaspoon/½ g freshly grated nutmeg
½ cup/118 ml honey or pure maple syrup
1 tablespoon/15 ml sunflower oil
½ teaspoon/2.5 ml pure vanilla extract
½ cup/61 g dried cranberries
½ cup/80 g golden raisins

Preheat the oven to 350°F/175°C and grease a large rimmed baking sheet.

Combine the oats, almonds, pecans, coconut, pumpkin seeds, cinnamon, and nutmeg in a large bowl. Combine the honey, oil, and vanilla in a small saucepan and heat until boiling. Pour the liquid over the dry ingredients. Stir to coat, then spread the mixture onto the baking sheet. Bake for 20 to 25 minutes, stirring once, or until golden brown.

Let the muesli cool for 15 minutes, then stir in the dried cranberries and golden raisins. Muesli stays fresh in an airtight container for about 2 weeks.

Oatmeal Molasses Bread

THIS IS THE GLUTEN-FREE VERSION of hearty whole wheat sandwich bread. The sorghum has a slightly sweet taste that is amplified by the molasses in the dough. The bread has a grainy texture similar to that of some wheat breads made with whole-grain flours, and the oats add additional textural interest. This is an interesting bread to turn into a stuffing for pork chops, too (see page 67 for a basic stuffing recipe).

MAKES 1 LOAF

- 2 tablespoons/30 g ground chia seeds
- 2¼ teaspoons/7 g active dry yeast
- 2 tablespoons/27 g firmly packed light brown sugar
- 1 cup/237 ml whole milk, heated to 110° to 115°F/43° to 46°C
- 1 cup/158 g brown rice flour, plus more if necessary
- ¾ cup/95 g sorghum flour
- ½ cup/85 g potato starch
- ¼ cup/31 g tapioca starch
- ¼ cup/30 g teff flour
- 1½ teaspoons/6 g gluten-free baking powder
- 1 teaspoon/9 g xanthan gum
- ½ teaspoon/3 g fine salt
- 3 large eggs, at room temperature
- ¼ cup/59 ml light molasses
- 3 tablespoons/42 g unsalted butter, melted and cooled
- ¾ cup/72 g gluten-free old-fashioned rolled oats, divided

Spray the inside of a 9 × 5-inch/23 × 11 cm loaf pan with vegetable oil spray.

Combine the chia seeds, yeast, brown sugar, and warm milk in the bowl of a stand mixer fitted with the paddle attachment and mix well. Set aside for about 10 minutes while the yeast proofs. Combine the 1 cup/158 g of rice flour and the

(recipe continues)

sorghum flour, potato starch, tapioca starch, teff flour, baking powder, xanthan gum, and salt in a deep mixing bowl and whisk well.

When the yeast looks frothy add the eggs, molasses, and melted butter and mix well. Add the dry ingredients and ½ cup/48 g of the oats and beat at medium speed until combined. Increase the speed to high and beat the dough for 3 to 5 minutes, or until it has the consistency of a thick cake batter that would require spreading in a cake pan; it is too thick to pour. Add more rice flour by 1 tablespoon/10 g amounts to make the dough thicker, if necessary.

Lightly grease the inside of a large mixing bowl with vegetable oil or softened butter. Scrape the dough out of the mixer bowl and into the greased bowl, smoothing the top with moistened fingers or a rubber spatula dipped in water. Place it in the bowl and turn it over once so it is lightly greased all over. Cover the bowl loosely with a sheet of oiled plastic wrap or a damp tea towel and place it in a warm, draft-free spot. Allow the dough to rise for 1 hour, or until it has doubled in bulk.

Punch down the dough and scrape it into the prepared pan. Smooth the top with a rubber spatula dipped in water, and cover the pan with a sheet of oiled plastic wrap or a damp tea towel. Allow the bread to rise in a warm place for 40 to 50 minutes, or until it reaches ½ inch/1.25 cm from the top of the pan. Sprinkle the dough with the remaining ¼ cup/24 g of oats.

Preheat the oven to 350°F/175°C toward the end of the rising time.

Covering the loaf loosely with aluminum foil after 30 minutes, bake the bread for 50 to 55 minutes, or until the bread is golden brown, the top is firm, and it has reached an internal temperature of 200°F/93°C on an instant-read thermometer. Remove the bread from the oven and allow it to cool for 30 minutes. Remove it from the loaf pan by running a spatula around the rim and invert it onto a cooling rack to cool completely.

NOTE:

The bread is best the day it is baked, but it can be stored refrigerated, tightly covered with plastic wrap, for up to 2 days.

VARIATION:

- Add 1 tablespoon/8 g of toasted sesame seeds to the dough, and substitute 1 teaspoon/5 ml of toasted sesame oil for 1 teaspoon/5 g of the melted butter.

Molasses is a delicious by-product that is extracted during the sugar cane refining process used to make sugar crystals. The sugar cane is crushed to remove the juice, which is then boiled vigorously. Machines utilize centrifugal force to extract the sugar crystals from the syrup. The remaining syrup becomes molasses. The flavor and color of molasses varies, depending on how early or late in the process the molasses is extracted. The molasses is where all the nutritional benefits of the cane sugar are found. One tablespoon/15 ml of molasses contains 40 percent of the daily recommendation for iron and 20 percent of the daily requirement of calcium. What is used most often in cooking is blackstrap molasses. It is the syrup remaining after the third extraction of sugar from sugar cane. *Blackstrap* (derived in part from the Dutch *stroop,* meaning syrup) refers to the liquid's dark color. It has a very strong, somewhat bittersweet flavor. (In Europe, blackstrap molasses is often referred to as dark or black treacle.) By measure, it is 55 percent sucrose, the least sweet of the varieties. Light molasses, which is 65 percent sucrose, is what remains after the first processing of the sugar. It is generally unsulfured and is the lightest as well as sweetest variety, which is why it's often used as a syrup for pancakes or stirred into hot cereals.

Caraway Potato Bread

THE INSPIRATION FOR THIS aromatic loaf is *Kartoffelbrot,* the traditional German potato bread made with both wheat and rye. There's a chewy hominess to its dense texture, and dotting it with caraway seeds makes it taste like a gluten-free version of rye bread. Many European cuisines have some variation on potato bread because the lowly potato, native to the New World, became a staple of peasant food across the Atlantic by the end of the sixteenth century. Some recipes today call for dried potato flakes instead of real mashed potatoes, but I don't think the results are as satisfying. A slice of this bread turns a bowl of thick vegetable soup into a truly satisfying meal.

MAKES 1 LOAF

1 (8-ounce/227 g) russet potato, peeled and cut into 1-inch/2.5 cm cubes
¾ cup/178 ml whole milk
4 tablespoons (½ stick)/56 g unsalted butter
¾ teaspoon/4.5 g salt
2¼ teaspoons/7 g active dry yeast
1 tablespoon/13 g granulated sugar
1¼ cups/198 g brown rice flour
¾ cup/95 g sorghum flour
⅔ cup/85 g cornstarch
½ cup/85 g potato starch
¼ cup/30 g garbanzo bean flour
2 tablespoons/8.5 g nonfat dried milk powder
1 teaspoon/9 g xanthan gum
1 tablespoon/7 g caraway seeds, divided
1 large egg, at room temperature
1 tablespoon/15 ml heavy whipping cream
1 tablespoon/18 g coarse sea salt

Spray the inside of a 9 × 5-inch/23 × 11 cm loaf pan with vegetable oil spray.

Place the potato in a saucepan and cover it by cold salted water by 1 inch/2.5 cm. Bring to a boil over high heat, then lower the heat to medium and cook, uncovered, for 12 to 15 minutes, or until the potato cubes are very tender when pierced by a paring knife. While the potato boils, combine the milk, butter, and salt in a small saucepan. Heat over low heat until the butter melts, stirring frequently.

Drain the potato, reserving ½ cup/118 ml of the water. Add the milk mixture to the potato and mash well, using a potato masher. Set aside.

Reheat the potato water, if necessary, to a temperature of 110° to 115°F/43° to 46°C. Combine the yeast, sugar, and potato water in the bowl of a stand mixer fitted with the paddle attachment and mix well. Set aside for about 10 minutes while the yeast proofs. Combine the rice flour, sorghum flour, cornstarch, potato starch, garbanzo bean flour, milk powder, and xanthan gum in a mixing bowl and whisk well.

When the yeast looks frothy add the mashed potato and beat at medium speed for 2 minutes. Add the dry ingredients and beat at medium speed until combined. Increase the speed to high and beat the dough for 3 to 5 minutes, or until it has the consistency of a thick cake batter that would require spreading in a cake pan; it is too thick to pour. Beat in 2 teaspoons/2.3 g of the caraway seeds.

Lightly grease the inside of a large mixing bowl with vegetable oil or softened butter. Scrape the dough out of the mixer bowl into the greased bowl, smoothing the top with moistened fingers or a rubber spatula dipped in water. Cover the bowl loosely with a sheet of oiled plastic wrap or a damp tea towel and place it in a warm, draft-free spot. Allow the dough to rise for 1 hour, or until it has doubled in bulk. Punch down the dough.

Scrape the dough into the prepared pan, smooth the top with a rubber spatula dipped in water, and cover the pan with a sheet of oiled plastic wrap or a damp tea towel. Allow the bread to rise in a warm place for 40 to 50 minutes, or until it reaches ½ inch/1.25 cm from the top of the pan.

Preheat the oven to 375°F/190°C toward the end of the rising time.

(recipe continues)

Beat the egg and cream together in a small bowl and brush the egg mixture on the top of the loaf. Sprinkle the remaining caraway seeds and coarse salt over the egg mixture.

Covering the loaf loosely with aluminum foil after 30 minutes, bake the bread for 50 to 55 minutes, or until the bread is golden brown, the top is firm, and it has reached an internal temperature of 195°F/91°C on an instant-read thermometer. Remove the bread from the oven and allow it to cool for 30 minutes. Remove it from the loaf pan by running a spatula around the rim and invert it onto a cooling rack to cool completely.

NOTE:

The bread is best the day it is baked, but it can be stored refrigerated, tightly covered with plastic wrap, for up to 2 days.

VARIATION:

- Substitute fennel seeds for the caraway seeds, and add 1 teaspoon/0.8 g of fresh thyme or ½ teaspoon/0.7 g of dried to the dough.

Garlicky Garbanzo Bean and Herb Bread

THIS HEARTY AND AROMATIC BREAD was inspired by my love of hummus. Garbanzo bean flour really does give loaves a bean flavor, and the addition of heady garlic and herbs balances that nicely. This is a great bread to use for grilled cheese sandwiches, and the flavors pair very well with the nuttiness of Gruyère or the earthiness of Manchego. If you have any left over, turn it into croutons for your next Caesar salad or top a bowl of split pea soup.

MAKES 1 LOAF

¼ cup/59 ml olive oil
4 garlic cloves, minced
1 large shallot, minced
1 tablespoon/5 g chopped fresh oregano (substitute 1 teaspoon/1.8 g dried)
2 teaspoons chopped fresh rosemary (substitute ½ teaspoon/0.6 g dried)
2 tablespoons/30 g ground chia seeds
1 tablespoon/12 g active dry yeast
2 tablespoons/27 g firmly packed light brown sugar
1 cup/237 ml water, heated to 110° to 115°F/43° to 46°C
1¾ cups/90 g garbanzo bean flour
1½ cups/187.5 g tapioca flour
¾ cup/96 g cornstarch
⅔ cup/105 g brown rice flour
1½ teaspoons/13.5 g xanthan gum
1 teaspoon/6 g fine salt
3 large eggs, at room temperature

Spray the inside of a 9 × 5-inch/23 × 11 cm loaf pan with vegetable oil spray.

(*recipe continues*)

Heat the oil in a small saucepan over medium heat. Add the garlic and shallot and cook, stirring frequently, for 3 minutes, or until the shallot is translucent. Add the oregano and rosemary and cook for 30 seconds. Set aside to cool.

Combine the chia seeds, yeast, brown sugar, and water in the bowl of a stand mixer fitted with the paddle attachment and mix well. Set aside for about 10 minutes while the yeast proofs. Combine the garbanzo bean flour, tapioca flour, cornstarch, brown rice flour, xanthan gum, and salt in a deep mixing bowl and whisk well.

When the yeast looks frothy add the eggs and the garlic mixture and mix well. Add the dry ingredients and beat at medium speed until combined. Increase the speed to high and beat the dough for 3 to 5 minutes, or until it has the consistency of a thick but still pourable cake batter.

Scrape the dough into the prepared pan, smooth the top with a rubber spatula dipped in water, and cover the pan with a sheet of oiled plastic wrap or a damp tea towel. Allow the bread to rise in a warm place for 40 to 50 minutes, or until it reaches ½ inch/1.25 cm from the top of the pan.

Preheat the oven to 375°F/190°C toward the end of the rising time.

Covering the loaf loosely with aluminum foil after 30 minutes, bake the bread for 45 to 50 minutes, or until the bread is golden brown, the top is firm, and it has reached an internal temperature of 195°F/91°C on an instant-read thermometer. Remove the bread from the oven and allow it to cool for 30 minutes. Remove it from the loaf pan by running a spatula around the rim and invert it onto a cooling rack to cool completely.

NOTE:

The bread is best the day it is baked, but it can be stored refrigerated, tightly covered with plastic wrap, for up to 2 days.

VARIATIONS:

- Add ½ cup/130 g of chopped roasted red bell pepper to the dough.
- Substitute 1 teaspoon/2.5 g of ground cumin and 1 teaspoon/2 g of ground coriander for the oregano and rosemary.

Garlic is classified as both a food and medicinal herb. Numerous large studies have shown garlic can significantly lower LDL cholesterol levels without hurting beneficial HDL cholesterol levels, by blocking the liver from making too much LDL cholesterol. There is also some evidence that garlic can mildly lower blood pressure by dilating or expanding blood vessels. And garlic helps prevent blood clots—and therefore reduces the risk of heart attack and stroke—by decreasing the stickiness of platelets.

Sesame Scallion Bread

ASIAN RESTAURANTS are havens for those on a gluten-free diet because rice is the major grain used, and most frequently dishes are thickened with cornstarch instead of wheat flour. One exception, however, are fried scallion pancakes, which is one of my favorite treats. When I fry them at home, I frequently add aromatic sesame oil to the pan. That dish is the inspiration for this bread, which I use for sandwiches stuffed with mildly flavored foods, such as chicken or turkey. It's in those cases that the bread can truly become the star of the dish.

MAKES 1 LOAF

2¼ teaspoons/7 g active dry yeast

2 tablespoons/27 g firmly packed light brown sugar

¾ cup/178 ml water, heated to 110° to 115°F/43° to 46°C

2 tablespoons/30 ml toasted sesame oil

2 tablespoons/27 g unsalted butter

¼ cup/32 g sesame seeds, divided

⅔ cup/80 g millet flour

½ cup/60 g garbanzo bean flour

⅓ cup/43 g cornstarch

½ cup/56 g almond meal

⅓ cup/42 g tapioca flour

1 teaspoon/2 g unflavored gelatin or agar powder

1 teaspoon/9 g xanthan gum

½ teaspoon/3 g fine salt

3 large eggs, at room temperature, divided

4 scallions, white parts, and 4 inches/8 cm of green tops, chopped

Spray the inside of an 8½ × 4½-inch/21.25 × 9.25 cm loaf pan with vegetable oil spray.

(recipe continues)

Combine the yeast, brown sugar, and ½ cup/118 ml of the warm water in the bowl of a stand mixer fitted with the paddle attachment and mix well. Set aside for about 10 minutes while the yeast proofs.

Heat the sesame oil and butter in a small skillet over medium-low heat. Reserve 1 tablespoon/8 g of the sesame seeds and add the remaining 3 tablespoons/24 g to the skillet. Cook, stirring frequently, for 2 minutes, or until the seeds are brown. Set aside.

Combine the millet flour, garbanzo bean flour, cornstarch, almond meal, tapioca flour, gelatin, xanthan gum, and salt in a deep mixing bowl and whisk well.

When the yeast looks frothy add the remaining ¼ cup/60 ml of warm water, 2 of the eggs, and the sesame seed mixture and mix well. Add the dry ingredients and beat at medium speed until combined. Increase the speed to high and beat the dough for 3 to 5 minutes, or until it has the consistency of a thick but still pourable cake batter. Beat in the scallions.

Scrape the dough into the prepared pan, smooth the top with a rubber spatula dipped in water, and cover the pan with a sheet of oiled plastic wrap or a damp tea towel. Allow the bread to rise in a warm place for 40 to 50 minutes, or until it reaches ½ inch/1.25 cm from the top of the pan.

Preheat the oven to 425°F/215°C toward the end of the rising time.

Whisk the remaining egg with 2 teaspoons/10 ml of water and a pinch of salt. Brush the egg wash on top of the bread and sprinkle it with the remaining sesame seeds. Covering the loaf loosely with aluminum foil after 20 minutes, bake the bread for 50 to 55 minutes, or until the bread is golden brown, the top is firm, and it has reached an internal temperature of 190°F/87°C on an instant-read thermometer. Remove the bread from the oven and allow it to cool for 30 minutes. Remove it from the loaf pan by running a spatula around the rim and invert it onto a cooling rack to cool completely.

NOTE:

The bread is best the day it is baked, but it can be stored refrigerated, tightly covered with plastic wrap, for up to 2 days.

Sesame seeds add more than delicious flavor to foods. These tiny seeds grown in almost all tropical regions are a very good source of copper and magnesium. Copper, which contains many anti-inflammatory components, is known for its use in reducing some of the pain and swelling of rheumatoid arthritis, an autoimmune disease. Magnesium is important in the functioning of both our respiratory and vascular systems. Studies have shown that magnesium can help to lower blood pressure as well as preventing airway spasms for those suffering from asthma.

French Baguette

CRISPY ON THE OUTSIDE and light and airy on the inside is what we expect from a French bread, and this baguette fits the bill. Just say the word *baguette* and you conjure up a picture in your mind of a young French *garçon* in stripes strolling down the street with a few loaves tucked into his elbow. It goes with anything and everything. It's never made at home in France because the French are dedicated to the morning task of a trip to the *boulangerie*. But if you want a great gluten-free baguette, you do have to make it yourself, and this is your recipe to do it. If you want an even crisper crust, just leave it in the oven about five minutes longer.

MAKES 1 LOAF

- 2 tablespoons/30 g ground chia seeds
- 2¼ teaspoons/7 g active dry yeast
- 1 tablespoon/13 g granulated sugar
- 1 cup/237 ml water, heated to 110° to 115°F/43° to 46°C, divided
- ⅔ cup/80 g millet flour, plus more if needed
- ½ cup/60 g garbanzo bean flour
- ⅓ cup/43 g cornstarch
- ⅓ cup/57 g potato starch
- ¼ cup/31 g tapioca flour
- ¾ teaspoon/6.75 g xanthan gum
- ½ teaspoon/3 g fine salt
- 1 tablespoon/15 g unsalted butter, melted
- 1 tablespoon/10 g poppy seeds (optional)

Grease the inside of a long French baguette pan with vegetable oil or softened butter.

Combine the chia seeds, yeast, sugar, and ½ cup/118 ml of the warm water in the bowl of a stand mixer fitted with the paddle attachment and mix well. Set aside for about 10 minutes while the yeast proofs. Combine the ⅔ cup/80 g of millet flour

(*recipe continues*)

and the garbanzo bean flour, cornstarch, potato starch, tapioca flour, xanthan gum, and salt in a deep mixing bowl and whisk well.

When the yeast looks frothy add the remaining ½ cup/118 ml of warm water and the melted butter and mix well. Add the dry ingredients and beat at medium speed until combined. Increase the speed to high and beat the dough for 3 to 5 minutes, or until the dough has the consistency of a drop biscuit dough. Add more millet flour by 1 tablespoon/10 g amounts if necessary.

Scrape the dough evenly into the prepared pan, forming it into a long line. Cover the pan loosely with a sheet of oiled plastic wrap or a damp tea towel and allow the dough to rise for 1 hour in a warm spot, or until it has doubled in bulk. Sprinkle the top of the loaf with poppy seeds, if using.

Place the oven racks in the middle and lowest positions. Place a rimmed baking sheet on the lower rack and place a pizza stone on the upper rack. Preheat the oven to 400°F/200°C toward the end of the rising time, bring a kettle of water to a boil, and have a spray bottle of water handy.

Pour 1 cup/237 ml of boiling water into the heated sheet pan and slide the bread pan on top of the heated pizza stone. Spray the walls of the oven with the spray bottle, close the oven door and wait 30 seconds, then spray the oven walls again. Covering the loaf loosely with aluminum foil after 20 minutes, bake the bread for 45 to 50 minutes, or until the bread is golden brown, sounds hollow and thumps when tapped on the bottom, and has reached an internal temperature of 200°F/93°C on an instant-read thermometer. Remove the bread from the oven and allow it to cool for 30 minutes before slicing.

NOTE:

The bread is best the day it is baked, but it can be stored refrigerated, tightly covered with plastic wrap, for up to 2 days.

If you go to a French bakery, the number of names given to basically the same bread can be mind-boggling. It all depends on the size and shape. A *baguette* is long and thin, generally 24 inches/61 cm by 2 inches/5 cm, whereas a *bâtard* is shorter and wider; it's 16 inches/40.6 cm by 3 inches/8 cm. A long loaf shrinks in length even more when it becomes a *ficelle,* which is only a foot long and about 2 inches/5 cm wide. Round shapes are just as numerous. A large round or oval is dubbed a *pain de ménage* or a *pain boulot,* whereas smaller rounds are *boules* and rolls are *petits pains.*

Sourdough Boule

YOU CAN'T BAKE A LOAF of sourdough bread on a whim because of the time it takes to cultivate the wild yeast starter, but if you have a batch on hand already, this is a wonderful way to use it. The combination of millet flour and garbanzo bean flour enhances the natural tangy flavor that the bread gets from its fermented starter. There's a tangy flavor to sourdough bread, and that seems to play off and amplify all the savory flavors of the foods with which it's served.

MAKES 1 LOAF

2 tablespoons/30 g ground chia seeds
¼ cup/1.2 ml warm water
⅔ cup/80 g millet flour, plus more if needed
⅓ cup/40 g garbanzo bean flour
⅓ cup/43 g cornstarch
⅓ cup/57 potato starch
1 tablespoon/13 g granulated sugar
1¾ teaspoons/15.75 g xanthan gum
½ teaspoon/3 g fine salt
1 cup/237 ml Active Sourdough Starter (page 49)
1 large egg, at room temperature

Cover a baking sheet with parchment paper or a silicone baking mat.

Combine the chia seeds and water in the bowl of a stand mixer fitted with the paddle attachment and mix well. Set aside for about 10 minutes. Combine the ⅔ cup/80 g of millet flour and the garbanzo bean flour, cornstarch, potato starch, sugar, xanthan gum, and salt in a deep mixing bowl and whisk well.

Add the sourdough starter and egg to the mixer bowl and mix well. Add the dry ingredients and beat at medium speed until combined. Increase the speed to high and beat the dough for 3 to 5 minutes, or until the dough holds together and has the

(recipe continues)

consistency of a drop biscuit dough. Add more millet flour by 1 tablespoon/10 g amounts if necessary.

Form the dough into a mound 3 inches/7.5 cm high on the prepared baking sheet. Cover the bread loosely with a sheet of oiled plastic wrap and allow the dough to rise for 4 to 6 hours in a warm spot, or until it has doubled in bulk.

Place the oven racks in the middle and lowest positions. Place a rimmed baking sheet on the lower rack and place a pizza stone on the upper rack. Preheat the oven to 400°F/200°C toward the end of the rising time, bring a kettle of water to a boil, and have a spray bottle of water handy.

Pour 1 cup/237 ml of boiling water into the heated sheet pan and slide the baking sheet on top of the heated pizza stone. Spray the walls of the oven with the spray bottle, close the oven door and wait 30 seconds, then spray the oven walls again.

Covering the loaf loosely with aluminum foil after 20 minutes, bake the bread for 45 to 50 minutes, or until the bread is golden brown, sounds hollow and thumps when tapped on the bottom, and has reached an internal temperature of 200°F/93°C on an instant-read thermometer. Remove the bread from the oven and allow it to cool for 30 minutes before slicing.

NOTE:

The bread is best the day it is baked, but it can be stored refrigerated, tightly covered with plastic wrap, for up to 2 days.

When members of the Boudin family, who were master bakers in their native France, arrived in California during the gold rush, they found out that the sourdough culture there was very unique, and they became very famous for their bread with this special flavor. Miners flocked to their bakery every morning. The starter has been kept alive since 1849. They call it "mother dough" and always use the same recipe for the bread: flour, water, a pinch of salt, and some of the "mother dough." In fact, a member of the family saved the "mother dough" during the Great San Francisco Earthquake of 1906.

Ciabatta

IT'S DIFFICULT TO SHAPE gluten-free bread dough, which is why the majority of the recipes in this book are baked in pans rather than free form. The dough has the tendency to spread out like a brownie batter; however, ciabatta, an Italian bread, is typically rather flat, and the crispy crust of this loaf is delicious. Ciabatta, pronounced *chyah-BAH-tah,* literally means "slipper" in Italian and was first produced in Liguria, but almost every region has a variation. One of the reasons for its popularity is its shape; a square of ciabatta is perfect to slice open and use for a sandwich. This recipe is drawn from the Tuscan heritage and includes a bit of olive oil, and the top of the loaf is sprinkled with both sesame seeds and coarse salt.

MAKES 1 LOAF

2 tablespoons/16 g coarse gluten-free cornmeal
1 tablespoon/12 g active dry yeast
1 tablespoon/13 g granulated sugar
⅔ cup/158 ml water, heated to a temperature of 110° to 115°F/43° to 46°C, divided
1 cup/158 g brown rice flour, plus more if needed
¾ cup/90 g millet flour
⅔ cup/85 g cornstarch
¼ cup/42.5 g potato starch
¼ cup/28 g defatted soy flour
1 teaspoon/2 g unflavored gelatin or agar powder
1¼ teaspoons/11.25 g xanthan gum
¾ teaspoon/4.5 g fine salt
2 large eggs, at room temperature, divided
3 tablespoons/45 ml olive oil
2 tablespoons/16 g sesame seeds
1 tablespoon/18 g coarse sea salt

Line a baking sheet with parchment paper or a silicone baking mat. Sprinkle the cornmeal in a line in the center of the baking sheet.

Combine the yeast, sugar, and ⅓ cup/79 ml of the warm water in the bowl of a stand mixer fitted with the paddle attachment and mix well. Set aside for about 10 minutes while the yeast proofs. Combine the 1 cup/158 g of rice flour and the millet flour, cornstarch, potato starch, soy flour, gelatin, xanthan gum, and salt in a deep mixing bowl and whisk well.

When the yeast looks frothy add the remaining ⅓ cup/79 ml of warm water, 1 of the eggs, and olive oil and mix well. Add the dry ingredients and beat at medium speed until combined. Increase the speed to high and beat the dough for 3 to 5 minutes, or until the dough holds together and has the consistency of a drop biscuit dough. Add more rice flour by 1 tablespoon/10 g amounts, if necessary.

Form the dough into a log about 14 inches/35.5 cm long on top of the cornmeal on the baking sheet. Beat the remaining egg with 2 teaspoons/10 ml of water. Brush the top and sides of the loaf with the egg wash, and sprinkle with the sesame seeds and coarse salt. Cover the loaf with a sheet of oiled plastic wrap and allow the bread to rise in a warm place for 30 to 40 minutes, or until doubled in size.

Cut 3 diagonal slits ½ inch/1.25 cm deep along the top of the loaf with a sharp paring knife.

Place the oven racks in the middle and lowest positions. Place a rimmed baking sheet on the lower rack and place a pizza stone on the upper rack. Preheat the oven to 400°F/200°C toward the end of the rising time, bring a kettle of water to a boil, and have a spray bottle of water handy.

Pour 1 cup/237 ml of boiling water into the heated sheet pan and slide the baking sheet on top of the heated pizza stone. Spray the walls of the oven with the spray bottle, close the oven door and wait 30 seconds, then spray the oven walls again.

Bake the bread for 15 minutes, then cover it loosely with aluminum foil and lower the oven temperature to 375°F/190°C. Bake for an additional 20 to 25

(recipe continues)

minutes, or until the bread is golden brown, sounds hollow and thumps when tapped, and has reached an internal temperature of 200°F/93°C on an instant-read thermometer. Remove the bread from the oven and allow it to cool for 30 minutes before slicing.

NOTE:

The bread is best the day it is baked, but it can be stored refrigerated, tightly covered with plastic wrap, for up to 2 days.

VARIATIONS:

- Work ½ cup/40 g of freshly grated Parmesan cheese into the dough, omit the sea salt topping, and sprinkle the unbaked loaf with an additional 3 tablespoons/15 g of freshly grated Parmesan.
- Add 3 tablespoons/11 g of chopped fresh parsley, 1 tablespoon/2.5 g of chopped fresh basil, and 2 minced garlic cloves to the dough.

SAUSAGE AND APPLE CIABATTA STRATA

In the past decade or so, a whole category of savory bread puddings called *strata* have become popular brunch dishes, and I can understand why. There are endless variations on the theme of bread, eggs, and cheese, and the whole thing can be assembled the evening before. This one, featuring apples, raisins, and sausage, is one of my favorites. Ciabatta is a great bread to use in strata because it has a mild flavor and allows the added ingredients to shine.

SERVES 6 TO 8

- 8 large eggs
- 3 cups/725 ml whole milk
- Salt and freshly ground black pepper as desired
- 1 cup/113 g grated whole-milk mozzarella cheese
- 1 (¾-pound/340 g) loaf Ciabatta, cut into ¾-inch cubes
- 1 cup/145 g raisins
- ¾ pound/336 g bulk breakfast sausage
- 2 tablespoons/27 g unsalted butter
- 1 small onion, diced
- 1 large Golden Delicious or Granny Smith apple, peeled, cored, quartered, and diced
- 3 tablespoons/38 g granulated sugar
- 2 tablespoons/4 g chopped fresh sage (substitute 1 tablespoon/2 g dried)
- ½ teaspoon/1.15 g ground cinnamon

Preheat the oven to 350°F/175°C and grease a 13 × 9-inch/33 × 23-cm baking pan.

Combine the eggs, milk, salt, and pepper in a large mixing bowl and whisk well. Add the cheese, bread, and raisins and stir well. Press down so that the bread absorbs the liquid.

Heat a skillet over medium-high heat. Crumble the sausage into the skillet, breaking up any lumps with a fork. Cook the sausage, stirring frequently, for 5 minutes, or

(*recipe continues*)

until browned and no longer pink. Remove the sausage from the skillet with a slotted spoon and set aside.

Return the skillet to the stove and lower the heat to medium. Add the butter and onion. Cook, stirring frequently, for 3 minutes, or until the onion is translucent. Add the apple, sugar, sage, and cinnamon to the skillet. Cook, stirring frequently, for 3 to 5 minutes, or until the apple softens. Stir the sausage and apple mixture into the bread.

Transfer the mixture to the prepared pan. Cover the pan with aluminum foil and bake in the center of the oven for 30 minutes. Remove the foil and bake for an additional 15 to 20 minutes, or until a toothpick inserted into the center comes out clean and the top is lightly browned. Allow the strata to cool for 5 minutes before serving.

NOTE:

The strata can be prepared for baking up to 2 days in advance and refrigerated, tightly covered. Allow it to sit at room temperature for 1 hour before baking.

White Toasting Bread

LONG BEFORE THE ADVENT of Wonder Bread and all of its contemporaries, there was always a place in homes and on restaurant menus for a loaf of white bread that sliced easily to use in delicate finger sandwiches and could be toasted to use with butter and jam at breakfast, or used to line the sides of a charlotte mold for dessert. In writing this book, one of my quests was to develop such a bread, and it had to make great toasted bread-crumbs, too. This bread is mildly flavored and has a lovely denseness and richness to it, and, because of the dairy content, it has enough protein to toast up well, too.

MAKES 1 LOAF

2¼ teaspoons/7 g active dry yeast
1 tablespoon/13 g granulated sugar
1½ cups/355 ml whole milk, heated to 110° to 115°F/43° to 46°C, divided
1 cup/158 g white rice flour
1 cup/127 g sorghum flour
⅔ cup/85 g cornstarch
⅓ cup/57 g potato starch
2 tablespoons/14 g defatted soy flour
2 tablespoons/8.5 g nonfat dried milk powder
1¼ teaspoons/11.25 g xanthan gum
½ teaspoon/3 g fine salt
1 large egg, at room temperature
1 large egg white, at room temperature
2 tablespoons/27 g unsalted butter, melted and cooled
3 tablespoons/45 ml honey
1 teaspoon/5 ml cider vinegar

Spray the inside of an 8½ × 4½-inch/21.25 × 9.25 cm loaf pan with vegetable oil spray.

Combine the yeast, sugar, and ¼ cup/59 ml of the warm milk in the bowl of a stand mixer fitted with the paddle attachment and mix well. Set aside for about 10 minutes while the yeast proofs. Combine the rice flour, sorghum flour, cornstarch,

(recipe continues)

potato starch, soy flour, milk powder, xanthan gum, and salt in a mixing bowl and whisk well.

When the yeast looks frothy add the remaining 1¼ cups/296 ml of warm milk and the egg, egg white, melted butter, honey, and vinegar and mix well. Add the dry ingredients and beat at medium speed until combined. Increase the speed to high and beat the dough for 3 to 5 minutes, or until it has the consistency of a thick but still pourable cake batter.

Scrape the dough into the prepared pan, smooth the top with a rubber spatula dipped in water, and cover the pan with a sheet of oiled plastic wrap or a damp tea towel. Allow the bread to rise in a warm place for 40 to 50 minutes, or until it reaches ½ inch/1.25 cm from the top of the pan.

Preheat the oven to 375°F/190°C toward the end of the rising time.

Covering the loaf loosely with aluminum foil after 30 minutes, bake the bread for 45 to 50 minutes, or until the bread is golden brown, the top is firm, and it has reached an internal temperature of 190°F/87°C on an instant-read thermometer. Remove the bread from the oven and allow it to cool for 30 minutes. Remove it from the loaf pan by running a spatula around the rim and invert it onto a cooling rack to cool completely.

NOTE:

The bread is best the day it is baked, but it can be stored refrigerated, tightly covered with plastic wrap, for up to 2 days.

VARIATION:

- Substitute buttermilk for the whole milk, and bake the loaf for 50 to 55 minutes.

HOMEMADE BREADCRUMBS

And after talking about great breadcrumbs, here's your method to make them at home with White Toasting Bread.

MAKES 2 CUPS/216 G BREADCRUMBS

¼ pound/113 g sliced gluten-free white bread, preferably stale

Preheat the oven to 200°F/93°C and line a baking sheet with aluminum foil.

Spread the bread out in a single layer on the baking sheet, and bake for 1½ to 1¾ hours, or until totally dry. Remove the pan from the oven and allow the bread to cool.

Break the bread into 1-inch/2.5 cm cubes and grind them in a food processor fitted with the steel blade. Store the breadcrumbs in an airtight container.

NOTE:

The breadcrumbs will keep for up to 3 months.

VARIATIONS:

- This recipe creates what are called fresh breadcrumbs. For toasted breadcrumbs, bake the bread in a 375°F/190°C oven for 10 to 12 minutes per side, turning the slices with a spatula, or until browned.
- Italian breadcrumbs are toasted breadcrumbs that are then seasoned with parsley, other herbs, garlic, and Parmesan cheese. To create these at home, add 1 teaspoon/1 g of Italian seasoning, ½ teaspoon/1.5 g of granulated garlic, and 3 tablespoons/15 g of freshly grated Parmesan cheese to each 1 cup/108 g of plain breadcrumbs.

CHAPTER 3

Rich Loaves

The breads in this chapter could be deemed decadent. Many of them contain as much butter and as many eggs as a cake, which is why their mouthfeel is so luxurious. In fact, the quote from Marie Antoinette about the peasants is always given incorrectly. She didn't say, "Let them eat cake" when she heard the peasants were starving because they couldn't afford their usual coarse brown bread. What she said was, "Let them eat brioche," and, when you make this scrumptious brioche recipe, you'll see why it's been likened to cake ever since.

I believe there's a role that rich breads play in our lives. These are the loaves that are a treat to start the day or serve at a civilized afternoon tea. There's a recipe for challah, the ceremonial Jewish bread that is reserved for celebration of holidays and the Sabbath. And also included are a rich white bread and a few variations to elevate that basic formulation to a new level of delight.

When baking a bread with a rich dough, you have to keep a close eye on it as it bakes, especially when using gluten-free flours and starches, because the high percentage of protein in the eggs and butter produce the Maillard Reaction.

The Maillard Reaction is a culinary phenomenon that occurs when proteins in food are heated to temperatures of 310°F/154.4°C or higher, causing them to turn brown and achieve a richer flavor. It is named for famed French chemist Louis-Camille Maillard, who discovered the process at the start of the twentieth century. The browning reaction is similar to caramelization, but caramel is produced by the browning of sugars, while the molecules browned under the Maillard Reaction are proteins.

What this means is that the loaves will brown on the exterior long before the interior is cooked through. That is why most of these loaves are loosely covered with foil for at least some of the bake time.

Brioche

I'D TAKE BRIOCHE over a boule or baguette any day, if I have the choice. First mentioned in the early fifteenth century, this butter- and egg-enriched classic French bread, which is classified, along with the croissant, as *viennoiserie* (in the style of Vienna), is the epitome of richness and elegance. Use small toasted rounds of it under foie gras, or for the ultimate French toast soak slices of brioche in a sweetened egg bath. In the famed *Larousse Gastronomique,* the Bible of classic French cooking, it's also recommended to use the dough to create the crust of any sort of protein to be served *en croûte,* such as roasted beef, pâté, or salmon. It's actually very easy to make, and I've become so fond of the light texture of this gluten-free version that this is the only recipe I now use.

MAKES 1 LOAF

- 1 tablespoon/12 g active dry yeast
- 1 tablespoon/13 g granulated sugar
- ⅓ cup/79 ml water, heated to a temperature of 110° to 115°F/43° to 46°C
- 1⅓ cups/171 g cornstarch
- ⅓ cup/53 g brown rice flour
- ⅓ cup/42 g tapioca flour
- 1 teaspoon/2 g unflavored gelatin or agar powder
- 1½ teaspoons/13.5 g xanthan gum
- ½ teaspoon/3 g fine salt
- 4 large eggs, at room temperature, divided
- ⅔ cup/158 ml heavy whipping cream, at room temperature
- 6 tablespoons (¾ stick)/83 g unsalted butter, melted and cooled
- ¼ teaspoon/1.2 ml pure vanilla extract

Spray the inside of an 8½ × 4½-inch/21.25 × 9.25 cm loaf pan with vegetable oil spray.

(recipe continues)

Combine the yeast, sugar, and water in the bowl of a stand mixer fitted with the paddle attachment and mix well. Set aside for about 10 minutes while the yeast proofs. Combine the cornstarch, rice flour, tapioca flour, gelatin, xanthan gum, and salt in a deep mixing bowl and whisk well.

When the yeast looks frothy add 3 of the eggs and the cream, melted butter, and vanilla and mix well. Add the dry ingredients and beat at medium speed until combined. Increase the speed to high and beat the dough for 3 to 5 minutes, or until it has the consistency of a thick cake batter that would require spreading in a cake pan; it is too thick to pour.

Lightly grease the inside of a large mixing bowl with vegetable oil or softened butter. Scrape the dough out of the mixer bowl and into the greased bowl, smoothing the top with moistened fingers or a rubber spatula dipped in water. Cover the bowl loosely with a sheet of oiled plastic wrap or a damp tea towel and place it in a warm, draft-free spot. Allow the dough to rise for 1 hour, or until it has doubled in bulk.

Punch down the dough and scrape it into the prepared pan, smooth the top with a rubber spatula dipped in water, and cover the pan with a sheet of oiled plastic wrap or a damp tea towel. Allow the bread to rise in a warm place for 40 to 50 minutes, or until it reaches ½ inch/1.25 cm from the top of the pan. Beat the remaining egg with 2 teaspoons/10 ml of water and a pinch of salt. Brush the egg wash over the top of the loaf.

Preheat the oven to 350°F/175°C toward the end of the rising time.

Covering the loaf loosely with aluminum foil after 25 minutes, bake the bread for 45 to 50 minutes, or until the bread is golden brown, sounds hollow and thumps when tapped on the bottom, and has reached an internal temperature of 190°F/87°C on an instant-read thermometer. Remove the bread from the oven and allow it to cool for 30 minutes. Remove it from the loaf pan by running a spatula around the rim and invert it onto a cooling rack to cool completely.

NOTE:

The bread is best the day it is baked, but it can be stored refrigerated, tightly covered with plastic wrap, for up to 2 days.

VARIATION:

- Add ⅔ cup/97 g of raisins or some sort of chopped dried fruit mixture to the dough.

While dishes like bread pudding and French toast are naturals to make with this bread that's rich in both eggs and butter, I also use it in many more ways. For a richer coating for food to be oven-fried or pan-fried, use brioche to make your breadcrumbs. I also substitute brioche for English muffins to use for brunch dishes like eggs Benedict, and a thick slice of toasted brioche for dessert is as delicious as a shortcake when topped with fresh fruit and whipped cream.

CREOLE BREAD PUDDING

Creole Bread Pudding is one of my favorite dishes to make with brioche because it has such inherent richness. Pecans and raisins dot this rich, cinnamon-scented pudding from the New Orleans tradition; because it's a way to use up stale bread, it was a "peasant dish" until the twentieth century.

MAKES 6 TO 8 SERVINGS

½ cup/54 g chopped pecans
5 large eggs
1 cup/202 g granulated sugar
2 cups/200 ml whole milk
6 tablespoons (¾ stick)/83 g unsalted butter, melted
1½ teaspoons/7.4 ml pure vanilla extract
1 teaspoon/2 g ground cinnamon
Pinch of salt
½ pound/227 g loaf Brioche, cut into ½-inch/1.25 cm slices
½ cup/73 g raisins
½ to ¾ cup/118 to 178 ml gluten-free caramel sauce, purchased or homemade

Preheat the oven to 350°F/175°C and grease a 13 × 9-inch/33 × 23 cm baking dish with vegetable oil spray or melted butter.

Spread the pecans in a single layer on a rimmed baking sheet and toast for 5 to 7 minutes, or until lightly browned. Set aside.

Combine the eggs, sugar, milk, melted butter, vanilla, cinnamon, and salt in a mixing bowl and whisk well. Add the bread slices to the mixing bowl and press them down so that the bread will absorb the liquid. Stir in the raisins and pecans. Allow the mixture to sit for 10 minutes.

Transfer the mixture to the prepared pan. Cover the baking pan with aluminum foil and bake in the center of the oven for 30 minutes. Remove the foil and bake for an additional 15 to 20 minutes, or until puffed and an instant-read thermometer inserted into the center registers 165°F/74°C. Serve immediately, topped with caramel sauce.

VARIATIONS:

- Substitute maple syrup for the granulated sugar, reduce the cinnamon to ½ teaspoon/1 g, and substitute walnuts for the pecans.
- Substitute ¾ cup/178 ml of orange marmalade for ¾ cup/151 g of the sugar, omit the cinnamon and pecans, and substitute dried cranberries for the raisins.
- Serve topped with ice cream or sweetened whipped cream.

Challah

THE TRADITIONAL CHALLAH served at countless Jewish homes on Friday evenings to celebrate the start of the Sabbath is a long oval shape made by braiding strands of dough. Unfortunately, challah dough made with gluten-free ingredients is too soft to braid, but this Jewish ceremonial egg bread does have a nice design when baked in a Bundt pan. The eggs become the dominant flavor, and the dough is just slightly sweetened. Along with brioche, challah is one of my top choices for making French toast and bread pudding because the ingredients in the bread itself add more richness to the dishes.

MAKES 1 LOAF

1 tablespoon/12 g active dry yeast
2 teaspoons/8 g granulated sugar
1 cup/237 ml water, heated to 110° to 115°F/43° to 46°C, divided
1 cup/158 g brown rice flour
1 cup/120 g millet flour
⅔ cup/85 g cornstarch
⅓ cup/42 g tapioca flour
¼ cup/28 g defatted soy flour
1½ teaspoons/13.5 g xanthan gum
½ teaspoon/3 g fine salt
3 large eggs, at room temperature
1 large egg yolk, at room temperature
¼ cup/59 ml vegetable oil
3 tablespoons/45 ml honey

Spray the inside of a 9-inch/23 cm Bundt pan with vegetable oil spray.

Combine the yeast, sugar, and ¼ cup/59 ml of the warm water in the bowl of a stand mixer fitted with the paddle attachment and mix well. Set aside for about 10 minutes while the yeast proofs. Combine the rice flour, millet flour,

(recipe continues)

cornstarch, tapioca flour, soy flour, xanthan gum, and salt in a deep mixing bowl and whisk well.

When the yeast looks frothy add the remaining ¾ cup/178 of warm water and the eggs, egg yolk, oil, and honey and mix well. Add the dry ingredients and beat at medium speed until combined. Increase the speed to high and beat the dough for 3 to 5 minutes, or until it has the consistency of a thick but still pourable cake batter.

Scrape the dough into the prepared pan, smooth the top with a rubber spatula dipped in water, and cover the pan with a sheet of oiled plastic wrap or a damp tea towel. Allow the bread to rise in a warm place for 40 to 50 minutes, or until it reaches ½ inch/1.25 cm from the top of the pan.

Preheat the oven to 375°F/190°C toward the end of the rising time.

Covering the loaf loosely with aluminum foil after 30 minutes, bake the bread for 50 to 55 minutes, or until the bread is golden brown, the top is firm, and it has reached an internal temperature of 200°F/93°C on an instant-read thermometer. Remove the bread from the oven and allow it to cool for 30 minutes. Remove it from the loaf pan by running a spatula around the rim and invert it onto a cooling rack to cool completely.

NOTE:

The bread is best the day it is baked, but it can be stored refrigerated, tightly covered with plastic wrap, for up to 2 days.

VARIATION:

- Add ½/72.5 to ¾ cup/109 g of raisins to the dough.

There is no resource as authoritative as anything written by my friend Joan Nathan about Jewish food. We met many years ago in Washington, and her ninety-nine-year-old mother lives in Providence, so I get to see her often. Here's what she wrote about challah in her award-winning book *Jewish Cooking in America* (Knopf, 1998).

"There are two words for bread in Hebrew: *lechem* and *challah*. Lechem is the everyday bread. . . . Challah is the special, usually white egg bread reserved for the Sabbath. Challah is also the word that refers to the portion of dough set apart for the high priests in the Temple of Jerusalem. One of the three commandments incumbent upon women, 'taking challah,' evolved sometime following the destruction of the Temple by the Romans in 70 CE. Following the rising of the dough, women would separate a piece and burn it to remind them of the offerings to the Temple. For nearly two millennia it has symbolically replaced the sacrificial offerings. All challah that is baked today is kosher only if 'challah has been taken. . . .' It was the Eastern European immigrants who put challah on the gastronomical map in the country. In biblical times . . . Sabbath bread was probably more like our present-day pita. Through the ages and as Jews moved to different lands the loaves varied. But only in America could Jews eat challah . . . every day of the week. . . . Elsewhere a round challah at Rosh Hashanah became a symbol of life. Usually the Rosh Hashanah bread is formed in a circle, to signify the desire for a long life. At this point, local traditions diverge. Some people add saffron and raisins to make the bread just a little bit more special than a typical Friday-night loaf. In certain towns of Russia, the round challah was imprinted with the shape of a ladder on top, to symbolize the ascent to God on high. . . . Many challot traditions were lost as a result of the Holocaust or because of Soviet religious suppression. . . ."

White Sandwich Bread

FEW PEOPLE, INCLUDING ME, get terribly excited when someone mentions white bread. On one end of the spectrum it is spongy, and at the other end of the scale are breads with good texture but little inherent flavor. But here's the loaf you're looking for to toast in the morning or fill with some tasty salad and a few crisp lettuce leaves for your sandwich lunch. It's rich from both eggs and butter, but it's also sturdy enough for these tasks. The bread certainly takes a backseat position to the other foods with which it's joined, but it's pleasing in every way.

MAKES 1 LOAF

- 2¼ teaspoons/7 g active dry yeast
- 3 tablespoons/40 g firmly packed light brown sugar
- 1½ cups/355 ml water, heated to 110° to 115°F/43° to 46°C, divided
- ½ cup/62.5 g tapioca flour
- ¾ cup/90 g garbanzo bean flour
- 1 cup/170 g potato starch
- 1¼ cups/197.5 g white rice flour
- ½ cup/34 g nonfat dried milk powder
- ¾ teaspoon/6.75 g xanthan gum
- ½ teaspoon/3 g fine salt
- 3 large eggs, at room temperature
- 4 tablespoons (½ stick)/56 g unsalted butter, melted and cooled

Spray the inside of an 8½ × 4½-inch/21.25 × 9.25 cm loaf pan with vegetable oil spray.

Combine the yeast, brown sugar, and ½ cup/118 ml of the warm water in the bowl of a stand mixer fitted with the paddle attachment and mix well. Set aside for about 10 minutes while the yeast proofs. Combine the tapioca flour, garbanzo bean

(recipe continues)

flour, potato starch, rice flour, milk powder, xanthan gum, and salt in a deep mixing bowl and whisk well.

When the yeast looks frothy add the remaining 1 cup/237 ml of warm water and the eggs and melted butter and mix well. Mix in the dry ingredients and beat at medium speed until combined. Increase the speed to high and beat the dough for 3 to 5 minutes, or until the dough has the consistency of a thick but still pourable cake batter.

Scrape the dough into the prepared pan, smooth the top with a rubber spatula dipped in water, and cover the pan with a sheet of oiled plastic wrap or a damp tea towel. Allow the bread to rise in a warm place for 40 to 50 minutes, or until it reaches ½ inch/1.25 cm from the top of the pan.

Place the oven racks in the middle and lowest positions. Place a rimmed baking sheet on the lower rack and place a pizza stone on the upper rack. Preheat the oven to 400°F/200°C toward the end of the rising time, bring a kettle of water to a boil, and have a spray bottle of water handy.

Pour 1 cup/237 ml of boiling water into the heated sheet pan and slide the loaf pan on top of the heated pizza stone. Spray the walls of the oven with the spray bottle, close the oven door, and wait 30 seconds, then spray the oven walls again. Covering the loaf loosely with aluminum foil after 25 minutes, bake the bread for 50 to 55 minutes, or until the bread is golden brown, the top is firm, and it has reached an internal temperature of 190°F/87°C on an instant-read thermometer. Remove the bread from the oven and allow it to cool for 30 minutes. Remove it from the loaf pan by running a spatula around the rim and invert it onto a cooling rack to cool completely.

NOTE:

The bread is best the day it is baked, but it can be stored refrigerated, lightly covered with plastic wrap, for up to 2 days.

PARMESAN SHALLOT ROUNDS

Gluten-free hors d'oeuvres frequently present a problem because so many of them involve crackers or bread. Here is my favorite predinner nibble. It's an updated version of something my mother served fifty years ago, and they virtually disappear as soon as they're put out at a party.

MAKES 2 DOZEN ROUNDS

2 tablespoons/27 g unsalted butter
2 large shallots, minced
Salt and freshly ground black pepper
12 slices White Sandwich Bread (page 114)
¼ cup/59 ml Dijon mustard
¾ cup/178 ml mayonnaise
¾ cup/60 g freshly grated Parmesan cheese

Preheat the oven broiler and cover a baking sheet with heavy-duty aluminum foil.

Heat the butter in a small skillet over medium-high heat. Add the shallots and cook, stirring frequently, for 5 to 7 minutes, or until the shallots soften and are lightly browned. Season to taste with salt and pepper and scrape the shallots into a mixing bowl.

Cut 2 rounds out of each slice of bread, using a 2-inch/5 cm round cutter. Arrange the rounds on the baking sheet. Broil the bread 8 inches/20 cm from the broiler element for 1 minute, or until toasted. Remove the bread from the oven.

Turn over the bread slices and spread mustard on the untoasted side. Add the mayonnaise and Parmesan to the mixing bowl with the shallots, season to taste with salt and pepper, and stir well.

(recipe continues)

Spread 1½ teaspoons/7 g of the mixture on top of the mustard on each bread round. Broil the rounds for 1 to 2 minutes, or until the tops are brown and bubbly. Watch them carefully as they broil. Serve immediately.

NOTE:

The rounds can be made up to 2 days in advance and refrigerated, tightly covered; they can also be frozen for up to 2 months. Reheat chilled rounds in a preheated 350°F/175°C oven for 5 to 7 minutes, and frozen rounds for 10 to 12 minutes.

VARIATIONS:

- Add 1 tablespoon finely chopped fresh oregano or rosemary to the shallot mixture, or add 2 to 3 minced garlic cloves to the pan along with the shallots.
- Substitute black olive tapenade or tomato paste for the mustard.
- Substitute sharp Cheddar or Gruyère for the Parmesan.
- Sprinkle the tops of the rounds with crumbled cooked bacon before broiling them.

Portuguese Sweet Bread

THERE IS A LARGE POPULATION with Portuguese ancestry living in Rhode Island, as there was when I lived on Nantucket. The immigration took place when the whaling trade was prominent during the nineteenth century. Part of that heritage is this slightly sweet bread that is wonderful for sandwiches, especially those made with fillings bound with mayonnaise. In some ways, this bread is similar to Hawaiian sweet bread, which shows how the trade patterns and voyages for exploration united the world long before e-mail.

MAKES 1 LOAF

1 tablespoon/12 g active dry yeast
2 teaspoons/8 g granulated sugar
⅔ cup/158 ml whole milk, heated to 110° to 115°F/43° to 46°C
⅔ cup/80 g millet flour
½ cup/64 g sorghum flour
½ cup/64 g cornstarch
⅓ cup/57 g potato starch
⅓ cup/42 g tapioca flour
⅓ cup/23 g nonfat dried milk powder
1¼ teaspoons/11.25 g xanthan gum
¾ teaspoon/3 g baking soda
½ teaspoon/3 g fine salt
2 large eggs, at room temperature
1 large egg yolk, at room temperature
4 tablespoons (½ stick)/56 g unsalted butter, melted and cooled
2 tablespoons/30 ml honey
½ teaspoon/2.5 ml cider vinegar

Spray the inside of an 8½ × 4½-inch/21.25 × 9.25 cm loaf pan with vegetable oil spray.

Combine the yeast, sugar, and warm milk in the bowl of a stand mixer fitted with the paddle attachment and mix well. Set aside for about 10 minutes while

(recipe continues)

the yeast proofs. Combine the millet flour, sorghum flour, cornstarch, potato starch, tapioca flour, milk powder, xanthan gum, baking soda, and salt in a deep mixing bowl and whisk well.

When the yeast looks frothy add the eggs, egg yolk, melted butter, honey, and vinegar and mix well. Add the dry ingredients and beat at medium speed until combined. Increase the speed to high and beat the dough for 3 to 5 minutes, or until it has the consistency of a thick but still pourable cake batter.

Scrape the dough into the prepared pan, smooth the top with a rubber spatula dipped in water, and cover the pan with a sheet of oiled plastic wrap or a damp tea towel. Allow the bread to rise in a warm place for 40 to 50 minutes, or until it reaches ½ inch/1.25 cm from the top of the pan.

Preheat the oven to 375°F/190°C toward the end of the rising time.

Covering the loaf loosely with aluminum foil after 30 minutes, bake the bread for 50 to 55 minutes, or until the bread is golden brown, the top is firm, and it has reached an internal temperature of 200°F/93°C on an instant-read thermometer. Remove the bread from the oven and allow it to cool for 30 minutes. Remove it from the loaf pan by running a spatula around the rim and invert it onto a cooling rack to cool completely.

NOTE:

The bread is best the day it is baked, but it can be stored refrigerated, tightly covered with plastic wrap, for up to 2 days.

Cheddar Cheese Bread

THE AROMA WHEN THIS BREAD is baking is tantalizing, with a combination of yeast and cheese filling the kitchen. It's reminiscent of Welsh rarebit and cheese fondue. This turned out to be one of the most versatile recipes in this book. At the end of the recipe I've given many variations that include some of my favorite combinations with Cheddar, as well as other cheese choices that I've found successful the many times I've made this bread.

MAKES 2 LOAVES

- 2 tablespoons/30 g ground chia seeds
- 2¼ teaspoons/7 g active dry yeast
- 1 tablespoon/13 g granulated sugar
- 1¾ cups/425 ml whole milk, heated to 110° to 115°F/43° to 46°C, divided
- 1½ cups/237 g brown rice flour
- ½ cup/60 g millet flour
- ½ cup/62.5 g tapioca flour
- ½ cup/64 g cornstarch
- ¼ cup/17 g nonfat dried milk powder
- 1 teaspoon/2 g unflavored gelatin or agar powder
- 1½ teaspoons/13.5 g xanthan gum
- ½ teaspoon/3 g fine salt
- 3 large eggs, at room temperature
- 4 tablespoons (½ stick)/56 g unsalted butter, melted and cooled
- 6 ounces/170 g sharp Cheddar cheese, grated, divided

Spray the inside of two 8½ × 4½-inch/21.25 × 9.25 cm loaf pans with vegetable oil spray.

Combine the chia seeds, yeast, sugar, and 1 cup/237 ml of the warm milk in the bowl of a stand mixer fitted with the paddle attachment and mix well. Set aside for about 10 minutes while the yeast proofs. Combine the rice flour, millet flour, tapioca

(recipe continues)

flour, cornstarch, milk powder, gelatin, xanthan gum, and salt in a deep mixing bowl and whisk well.

When the yeast looks frothy add the remaining ¾ cup/188 ml of warm milk and the eggs and melted butter and mix well. Add the dry ingredients and beat at medium speed until combined. Increase the speed to high and beat the dough for 3 to 5 minutes, or until it has the consistency of a thick but still pourable cake batter. Stir in 1½ cups/125 g of the cheese.

Scrape the dough into the prepared pan, smooth the top with a rubber spatula dipped in water, and cover the pan with a sheet of oiled plastic wrap or a damp tea towel. Allow the bread to rise in a warm place for 40 to 50 minutes, or until it reaches ½ inch/1.25 cm from the top of the pan. Sprinkle the top of the bread with the remaining cheese.

Preheat the oven to 375°F/190°C toward the end of the rising time.

Covering the loaf loosely with aluminum foil after 30 minutes, bake the bread for 50 to 55 minutes, or until the bread is golden brown, sounds hollow and thumps when tapped on the bottom, and has reached an internal temperature of 195°F/91°C on an instant-read thermometer. Remove the bread from the oven and allow it to cool for 30 minutes. Remove it from the loaf pan by running a spatula around the rim and invert it onto a cooling rack to cool completely.

NOTE:

The bread is best the day it is baked, but it can be stored refrigerated, tightly covered with plastic wrap, for up to 2 days.

VARIATIONS:

- Add ½ cup/56 g to ¾ cup/84 g of crumbled cooked bacon to the dough and substitute bacon grease for the butter.
- Add 2 tablespoons/1 g of chopped fresh dill to the dough.
- Add ½ cup/42 g of finely chopped pimiento to the dough.
- Add ½ cup/27 g of finely chopped sun-dried tomatoes and 1 teaspoon/2 g of Italian seasoning to the dough.
- Substitute 3 ounces/85 g of Gruyère cheese for 3 ounces/85 g of the Cheddar.
- Substitute Gruyère cheese for the Cheddar, and add ½ cup/43 g of caramelized onions to the dough. Spread additional onions on top of the bread, along with the remaining cheese, before baking.

Vegetable oil spray is a wonderful way to keep foods such as cheese from becoming permanently bonded to your pans, but it also has a tendency to coat the counters, too. Open your dishwasher and place the pan to be coated on the open door before you spray it. That keeps the counters clean, and any excess spray washes away the next time you use the dishwasher.

Buttery Almond Bread

YOU GET THE DELICATE and intoxicating flavor of almonds in two forms in this wonderful tea bread, as well as the texture of them. I love this bread topped with a layer of mascarpone and sprinkled with candied fruit as part of a brunch or afternoon tea.

MAKES 1 LOAF

¾ cup/108 g chopped blanched almonds
2 tablespoons/30 g ground chia seeds
½ cup/106 g firmly packed light brown sugar, divided
2¼ teaspoons/7 g active dry yeast
¾ cup/178 ml whole milk, heated to 110° to 115°F/43° to 46°C
1 cup/158 g brown rice flour
¾ cup/84 g almond meal
⅔ cup/84.7 g sorghum flour
⅔ cup/80 g millet flour
⅔ cup/113 g potato starch
3 tablespoons/12.75 g nonfat dried milk powder
1 teaspoon/2 g unflavored gelatin or agar powder
1½ teaspoons/13.5 g xanthan gum
½ teaspoon/3 g fine salt
3 large eggs, at room temperature
6 tablespoons (¾ stick)/83 g unsalted butter, melted and cooled
¼ teaspoon/1.2 ml pure vanilla extract

Preheat the oven to 350°F/175°C and spray the inside of a 9 × 5-inch/23 × 11 cm loaf pan with vegetable oil spray. Place the chopped almonds on a baking sheet and toast them for 5 to 7 minutes, or until lightly browned.

Combine the chia seeds, 2 tablespoons/26.5 g of the brown sugar, yeast, and the warm milk in the bowl of a stand mixer fitted with the paddle attachment and mix well. Set aside for about 10 minutes while the yeast proofs. Combine the remaining 6 tablespoons/79.5 g of brown sugar and the rice flour, almond meal, sorghum flour, millet flour, potato starch, milk powder, gelatin, xanthan gum, and salt in a deep mixing bowl and whisk well. When the yeast looks frothy add the eggs, melted butter, and vanilla and mix well. Add the dry ingredients and beat at medium speed until combined. Increase the speed to high and beat the dough for 3 to 5 minutes, or until it has the consistency of a thick but still pourable cake batter. Stir in the almonds.

Scrape the dough into the prepared pan, smooth the top with a rubber spatula dipped in water, and cover the pan with a sheet of oiled plastic wrap or a damp tea towel. Allow the bread to rise in a warm place for 40 to 50 minutes, or until it reaches ½ inch/1.25 cm from the top of the pan.

Preheat the oven to 375°F/190°C toward the end of the rising time.

Covering the loaf loosely with aluminum foil after 30 minutes, bake the bread for 50 to 55 minutes, or until the bread is golden brown, the top is firm, and it has reached an internal temperature of 195°F/91°C on an instant-read thermometer. Remove the bread from the oven and allow it to cool for 30 minutes. Remove it from the loaf pan by running a spatula around the rim and invert it onto a cooling rack to cool completely.

NOTE:

The bread is best the day it is baked, but it can be stored refrigerated, tightly covered with plastic wrap, for up to 2 days.

VARIATIONS:

- Substitute hazelnut meal and hazelnuts or pecan meal and pecans for the almonds and almond meal in the dough.
- Add ½ to ¾ cup/60 to 90 g of finely chopped dried fruit or candied fruit to the dough.

Boston Brown Bread

DURING THE COLONIAL ERA, a lot more corn and rye than wheat was available for baking, and the Native Americans taught the Europeans how to tap maple trees to create syrup. It was back in the middle 1600s that Boston brown bread first made its appearance. Back then there were no bread ovens, so the breads were cooked by steaming them in the fireplace in a closed container. This dense and delicious loaf is baked, but it has all of the characteristics of the colonial original. It's sweet and rich, and there's a wonderful yeasty flavor both from the yeast itself and the beer added to the dough.

MAKES 2 LOAVES

2 tablespoons/30 g ground chia seeds
2¼ teaspoons/7 g active dry yeast
2 teaspoons/8 g granulated sugar
½ cup/118 ml water, heated to 110° to 115°F/43° to 46°C
1 cup/158 g brown rice flour
1 cup/127 g sorghum flour
1 cup/125 g tapioca flour
½ cup/64 g cornstarch
½ cup/64 g finely ground yellow cornmeal
1½ teaspoons/13.5 g xanthan gum
½ teaspoon/3 g fine salt
3 large eggs, at room temperature
1 cup/237 ml gluten-free beer, such as Redbridge or Bard's, at room temperature
8 tablespoons (1 stick)/110 g unsalted butter, melted and cooled
½ cup/118 ml pure maple syrup
½ cup/24 g gluten-free old-fashioned rolled oats

Spray the inside of two 8½ × 4½-inch/21.25 × 9.25 cm loaf pans with vegetable oil spray.

Combine the chia seeds, yeast, sugar, and water in the bowl of a stand mixer fitted with the paddle attachment and mix well. Set aside for about 10 minutes while

(recipe continues)

the yeast proofs. Combine the rice flour, sorghum flour, tapioca flour, cornstarch, cornmeal, xanthan gum, and salt in a deep mixing bowl and whisk well.

When the yeast looks frothy add the eggs, beer, melted butter, and maple syrup and mix well. Add the dry ingredients and beat at medium speed until combined. Increase the speed to high and beat the dough for 3 to 5 minutes, or until it has the consistency of a thick but still pourable cake batter.

Scrape the dough into the prepared pan, smooth the top with a rubber spatula dipped in water, and cover the pan with a sheet of oiled plastic wrap or a damp tea towel. Allow the bread to rise in a warm place for 40 to 50 minutes, or until it reaches ½ inch/1.25 cm from the top of the pan. Sprinkle the loaf with the oats.

Preheat the oven to 350°F/175°C toward the end of the rising time.

Covering the loaf loosely with aluminum foil after 30 minutes, bake the bread for 50 to 55 minutes, or until the bread is golden brown, the top is firm, and it has reached an internal temperature of 195°F/91°C on an instant-read thermometer. Remove the bread from the oven and allow it to cool for 30 minutes. Remove it from the loaf pan by running a spatula around the rim and invert it onto a cooling rack to cool completely.

NOTE:

The bread is best the day it is baked, but it can be stored refrigerated, tightly covered with plastic wrap, for up to 2 days.

VARIATION:

- Add ½ cup/89 g to ¾ cup/133 g of chopped dates or raisins to the dough.

Spiced Raisin Bread

RAISIN BREAD IS AN AMERICAN STANDARD. It's right next to the panoply of white breads in supermarkets and you'll always find it in bakeries, too. But not all raisin breads are created equal. And I'm in love with this one. In fact, there are times I bake this bread just to have it around for French toast and bread pudding. The Chinese five-spice powder, a mixture of cinnamon, anise, ginger, fennel, and pepper, has a far more complex and somewhat more assertive flavor than the cinnamon traditionally used in this sweetened bread. If you don't have any Chinese five-spice powder, use a combination of cinnamon and ginger, and grind some black pepper into the dough, too.

MAKES 2 LOAVES

2¼ teaspoons/7 g active dry yeast
⅔ cup/135 g granulated sugar, divided
1½ cups/355 ml water, heated to 110° to 115°F/43° to 46°C, divided
1¼ cups/198 g brown rice flour
¾ cup/90 g teff flour
¾ cup/93.75 g tapioca flour
¾ cup/127.5 g potato starch
½ cup/34 g nonfat dried milk powder
1 teaspoon/9 g xanthan gum
½ teaspoon/3 g fine salt
3 large eggs, at room temperature
6 tablespoons (¾ stick)/83 g unsalted butter, melted and cooled
½ teaspoon/2.5 ml pure vanilla extract
1 cup/145 g raisins
1½ teaspoons/3 g Chinese five-spice powder

Spray the inside of two 8½ × 4½-inch/21.25 × 9.25 cm loaf pans with vegetable oil spray.

Combine the yeast, 1 tablespoon/12 g of the sugar, and ¼ cup/59 ml of the warm water in the bowl of a stand mixer fitted with the paddle attachment and mix well.

(recipe continues)

Set aside for about 10 minutes while the yeast proofs. Combine the remaining scant ⅔ cup/122 g of sugar, rice flour, teff flour, tapioca flour, potato starch, milk powder, xanthan gum, and salt in a deep mixing bowl and whisk well.

When the yeast looks frothy add the remaining 1¼ cups/296 ml of warm water, and the eggs, melted butter, and vanilla and mix well. Mix in the dry ingredients and beat at medium speed until combined. Increase the speed to high and beat the dough for 3 to 5 minutes, or until the dough has the consistency of a thick but still pourable cake batter.

Scrape the dough into the prepared pan. Combine the raisins and Chinese five-spice powder in a small mixing bowl and toss well. Gently fold the mixture into the dough to achieve a marbled look. Smooth the top of the bread with a rubber spatula dipped in water and cover the pan with a sheet of oiled plastic wrap or a damp tea towel. Allow the bread to rise in a warm place for 40 to 50 minutes, or until it reaches ½ inch/1.25 cm from the top of the pan.

Preheat the oven to 350°F/175°C toward the end of the rising time.

Covering the loaf loosely with aluminum foil after 30 minutes, bake the bread for 50 to 55 minutes, or until the bread is golden brown, the top is firm, and it has reached an internal temperature of 200°F/93°C on an instant-read thermometer. Remove the bread from the oven and allow it to cool for 30 minutes. Remove it from the loaf pan by running a spatula around the rim and invert it onto a cooling rack to cool completely.

NOTE:

The bread is best the day it is baked, but it can be stored at room temperature, tightly covered with plastic wrap, for up to 2 days.

(recipe continues)

VARIATIONS:

- Substitute apple pie spice, pumpkin pie spice, or a combination of cinnamon, allspice, and nutmeg for the Chinese five-spice powder.
- Substitute dried currants, dried cherries, dried blueberries, chopped dried apricots, or some combination of dried fruit for the raisins.

While boron does not receive a lot of play, this trace mineral is crucial to your health because it promotes bone health, especially in postmenopausal women. Raisins are an excellent source of boron, and both raisins and their parent fruit—grapes—are very high in antioxidant phenols that boost your immune system. Researchers have found that ounce for ounce, raisins contain almost three times the amount of antioxidants as their original grape counterparts do. Ah, the wonders of dehydration at work again.

Brandied Dried Fruit Bread

THIS BREAD IS THE CLOSEST I ever come to baking something that could even resemble a fruitcake. As we all know, only one of those was made in the past century and it gets passed around for a month every year. That said, this is *not* a fruitcake. It's based on some European fruit breads that are popular around the holidays. It contains a great variety of fruits, all laced with heady brandy and ginger, and the bread itself is rich and flavorful. It also makes wonderful French toast if you have some left over.

MAKES 1 LOAF

½ cup/72 g dried currants
½ cup/80 g golden raisins
¼ cup/40 g dried cherries
¼ cup/33 g chopped dried apricots
2 tablespoons/21 g finely chopped crystallized ginger
⅓ cup/79 ml brandy
2¼ teaspoons/7 g active dry yeast
2 teaspoons/8 g granulated sugar
1 cup/237 ml whole milk, heated to 110° to 115°F/43° to 46°C
1 cup/158 g brown rice flour
⅔ cup/80 g millet flour
½ cup/62.5 g tapioca flour
½ cup/64 g cornstarch
2 tablespoons/8.5 g nonfat dried milk powder
1½ teaspoons/13.5 g xanthan gum
½ teaspoon/3 g fine salt
2 large eggs, at room temperature
8 tablespoons (1 stick)/110 g unsalted butter, melted and cooled
½ cup/118 ml honey
½ teaspoon/2.5 ml pure vanilla extract
½ cup/68 g slivered blanched almonds

Combine the dried currants, raisins, dried cherries, dried apricots, crystallized ginger, and brandy in a mixing bowl. Toss well and allow the fruit to macerate for at least 6 hours, or preferably overnight.

(*recipe continues*)

Spray the inside of a 9 × 5-inch/23 × 11 cm loaf pan with vegetable oil spray.

Combine the yeast, sugar, and warm milk in the bowl of a stand mixer fitted with the paddle attachment and mix well. Set aside for about 10 minutes while the yeast proofs. Combine the rice flour, millet flour, tapioca flour, cornstarch, milk powder, xanthan gum, and salt in a deep mixing bowl and whisk well.

When the yeast looks frothy add the eggs, melted butter, honey, and vanilla and mix well. Add the dry ingredients and beat at medium speed until combined. Increase the speed to high and beat the dough for 3 to 5 minutes, or until it has the consistency of a thick but still pourable cake batter.

Scrape the dough into the prepared pan, smooth the top with a rubber spatula dipped in water, and cover the pan with a sheet of oiled plastic wrap or a damp tea towel. Allow the bread to rise in a warm place for 40 to 50 minutes, or until it reaches ½ inch/1.25 cm from the top of the pan. Sprinkle the top of the loaf with the almonds.

Preheat the oven to 350°F/175°C toward the end of the rising time.

Covering the loaf loosely with aluminum foil after 30 minutes, bake the bread for 50 to 55 minutes, or until the bread is golden brown, the top is firm, and it has reached an internal temperature of 195°F/91°C on an instant-read thermometer. Remove the bread from the oven and allow it to cool for 30 minutes. Remove it from the loaf pan by running a spatula around the rim and invert it onto a cooling rack to cool completely.

NOTE:

The bread is best the day it is baked, but it can be stored refrigerated, tightly covered with plastic wrap, for up to 2 days.

VARIATION:

- Substitute rum for the brandy and substitute firmly packed dark brown sugar for the honey.

Crystallized ginger is fresh ginger that is preserved by being candied in sugar syrup. It's then tossed with coarse sugar. It's very expensive in little bottles in the spice aisle, but many health food stores and whole foods markets sell it in bulk. You can also make it easily yourself. Peel and thinly slice fresh ginger and boil it in a large saucepan for 35 minutes, or until tender. Drain it, reserving ¼ cup/60 ml of the water. Weigh the ginger and then add an equal weight of granulated sugar to the pan with the ginger and the reserved water. Bring it to a boil over medium heat, stirring occasionally. Cook the mixture for 15 to 20 minutes, stirring frequently, or until the water has evaporated. Transfer the ginger to a sheet of parchment paper or a silicone baking mat and spread it out in a single layer. Allow it to cool, then sprinkle it with additional granulated sugar and store it for up to 1 month in an airtight container.

CHAPTER 4

Flatbreads

When you're making a flatbread, you are getting in touch with the entire history of civilized man and his food. The first breads, baked perhaps thirty thousand years ago, were probably accidental combinations of pounded grains and water that were mixed together and landed on a hot rock in the fire. And many modern-day flatbreads have not changed radically from that primitive prototype.

In this chapter you'll find such flatbreads as Armenian *lavash,* Indian *chapati,* and Ethiopian *injera* that are still being made today yet stem from this prehistoric era.

Oven-baked flatbreads are relatively modern. First of all, it meant that the nomadic tribes who invented the ancient flatbreads had settled down in villages in which they took the time to build ovens. Ovens can bake more bread than can skillets or other stovetop methods, and in a shorter period of time, but they also tend to require more wood, coal, or dried dung, whatever the local fuel resource happens to be. That's why few of the breads in this chapter require you to preheat the oven. Most tell you to find a large nonstick griddle or skillet.

What is also interesting about flatbreads is that some of them are authentically gluten-free, not a gluten-free version of a wheat flatbread recipe. *Socca,* from the sunny south of France, is only made with garbanzo bean flour, and the teff in injera has been the main staple crop of Ethiopia for millennia.

Focaccia

FOCACCIA, PRONOUNCED *foe-KAH-cha,* is one of the breads I eat when I want to be in denial about my food choices. Just as a croissant is made with so much butter you don't need to add any, so focaccia dough is created with a nice dose of olive oil, which gives it a wonderful mouthfeel as you chew it. Split it for sandwiches, and it can also be topped in myriad ways and served as an hors d'oeuvre.

MAKES ONE 17 × 11-INCH/43 × 28 CM FOCACCIA

- 3 tablespoons/45 g ground chia seeds
- 6¾ teaspoons/21 g active dry yeast
- 1 tablespoon/13 g granulated sugar
- 2¼ cups/559 ml water, heated to 110° to 115°F/43° to 46°C, divided
- 2½ cups/316 g brown rice flour
- 1½ cups/187.5 g tapioca flour
- 2 cups/224 g defatted soy flour
- 1 cup/120 g millet flour
- 2½ teaspoons/22.5 g xanthan gum
- 1¼ teaspoons/7.5 g fine salt
- ⅔ cup/158 ml olive oil, divided
- Coarse salt and freshly ground black pepper for sprinkling

Combine the chia seeds, yeast, sugar, and 1 cup/237 ml of the water in the bowl of a stand mixer fitted with the paddle attachment and mix well. Set aside for about 10 minutes while the yeast proofs. Combine the rice flour, tapioca flour, soy flour, millet flour, xanthan gum, and salt in a deep mixing bowl and whisk well.

When the yeast looks frothy add the remaining 1¼ cups/322 ml of water and ⅓ cup/79 ml of the oil and mix well. Add the dry ingredients and beat at medium speed until combined. Increase the speed to high and beat the dough for 3 to 5 minutes, or

(*recipe continues*)

until it has the consistency of a thick cake batter that would require spreading in a cake pan; it is too thick to pour.

Lightly grease the inside of a large mixing bowl with olive oil. Scrape the dough out of the mixer bowl and into the greased bowl, smoothing the top with moistened fingers or a rubber spatula dipped in water. Cover the bowl loosely with a sheet of oiled plastic wrap or a damp tea towel and place it in a warm, draft-free spot. Allow the dough to rise for 1 hour, or until it has doubled in bulk.

Grease the inside of a 17 × 11-inch/43 × 28 cm rimmed baking sheet. Punch down the dough and press it into the prepared baking sheet. Cover the bread with a sheet of oiled plastic wrap and allow it to rise in a warm place for 30 to 40 minutes, or until doubled in bulk.

Preheat the oven to 450°F/230°C toward the end of the rising time. Make indentations in the dough at 1-inch/2.5 cm intervals with oiled fingertips. Drizzle the top of the bread with the remaining ⅓ cup/79 ml of the oil and sprinkle it with coarse salt and pepper, or use one of the toppings listed below.

Place the oven racks in the middle and lowest positions. Place a second rimmed baking sheet on the lower rack and place a pizza stone on the upper rack. Bring a kettle of water to a boil and have a spray bottle of water handy.

Pour 1 cup of boiling water into the heated sheet pan, and slide the baking sheet on top of the heated pizza stone. Spray the walls of the oven with the spray bottle, close the oven door, and wait 30 seconds, then spray the oven walls again.

Covering the pan loosely with aluminum foil after 15 minutes, bake the bread for 20 to 25 minutes, or until the bread is golden brown, the top is firm, and it has reached an internal temperature of 190°F/87°C on an instant-read thermometer. Remove the bread from the oven and allow it to cool for 30 minutes before slicing.

(recipe continues)

NOTE:

The bread is best the day it is baked, but it can be stored refrigerated, tightly covered with plastic wrap, for up to 2 days.

VARIATIONS:

- Garlic Focaccia: Soak 4 peeled and minced garlic cloves in the olive oil for 2 hours before making the dough. Either strain and discard garlic, or mince it and sprinkle over the dough if you really like things garlicky.
- Sun-Dried Tomato Focaccia: Sprinkle the top with ½ cup/55 g of chopped sun-dried tomatoes packed in olive oil.
- Onion Focaccia: Heat 3 tablespoons/45 ml of olive oil in a skillet over medium heat. Add 2 thinly sliced, large sweet onions and toss to coat the onions with the oil. Cook over low heat, covered, for 10 minutes. Uncover the pan, raise the heat to medium-high, and sprinkle the onions with granulated sugar, salt, and pepper. Cook the onions, stirring frequently, for 12 to 15 minutes, or until medium brown. Spread the onions on top of the dough.
- Parmesan Olive Focaccia: Sprinkle the top with ¾ cup/60 g of freshly grated Parmesan cheese and dot it with ⅔ cup/80 g of chopped, oil-cured black olives.
- Herb Focaccia: Sprinkle the top with ½ cup/17 g of chopped fresh herbs, such as rosemary, basil, or oregano, or some combination.

CROUTONS

Crunchy bits of toast on top of a salad add textural variety, and, for some recipes, such as Caesar Salad, they are absolutely necessary. They are also a snap to make with stale bread. Although some recipes call for sautéing them, I find it is much easier to bake them.

MAKES 3 CUPS/90 G CROUTONS

3 cups/105 g (½-inch/1.25 cm) cubed Focaccia

⅓ cup/79 ml olive oil

Salt and freshly ground black pepper to taste

Preheat the oven to 375°F/190°C and line a baking pan with heavy-duty aluminum foil.

Place the bread cubes in the baking pan, drizzle them with the olive oil, and sprinkle with salt and pepper. Toss the cubes to coat them evenly.

Bake the cubes for a total of 10 minutes, or until brown and crunchy, turning them with a spatula after 5 minutes. Remove the pan from the oven and allow the cubes to cool completely. Store in an airtight container or resealable plastic bag at room temperature.

NOTE:

The croutons can be prepared up to 1 week in advance and kept at room temperature in an airtight container.

VARIATIONS:

- Press 2 garlic cloves through a garlic press and stir the garlic into the oil.
- Rather than using Focaccia bread, substitute herb bread, olive bread, or multigrain bread.
- Toss the croutons with 1 tablespoon/3 g of Italian seasoning or herbes de Provence before baking.
- Toss the croutons with ¼ cup/20 g of freshly grated Parmesan cheese before baking.

Pizza Dough

WE USUALLY THINK OF PIZZA as a meal rather than a flatbread, but flatbread is clearly what it is. This particular crust formulation will give you a crust that is crunchy at the edges and chewy in the center. If you want to grill the pizza, you can start it in the oven and bake it for 8 to 10 minutes, or until it is stable, and then transfer it to the grill to finish baking.

MAKES TWO 12-INCH/30.5 CM PIZZAS

1½ teaspoons/6 g active dry yeast

1 teaspoon/5 ml honey

⅔ cup/158 ml water, heated to 110° to 115°F/43° to 46°C

¾ cup/96 g cornstarch

¼ cup/31 g tapioca flour

¼ cup/39.5 g brown rice flour, plus more for rolling

¼ cup/30 g teff flour

1¼ teaspoons/11.25 g xanthan gum

½ teaspoon/3 g fine salt

1 large egg, at room temperature, beaten lightly

2 tablespoons/30 ml olive oil

Combine the yeast, honey, and water in the bowl of a stand mixer fitted with the paddle attachment and mix well. Set aside for about 10 minutes while the yeast proofs. Combine the cornstarch, tapioca flour, brown rice flour, teff flour, xanthan gum, and salt in a deep mixing bowl and whisk well.

When the yeast looks frothy add the egg and olive oil and mix well. Add the dry ingredients and beat at medium speed until combined. Increase the speed to high and beat the dough for 3 to 5 minutes, or until the dough has the consistency of a thick cake batter that would require spreading in a cake pan; it is too thick to pour.

Lightly grease the inside of a large mixing bowl with olive oil. Scrape the dough out of the mixer bowl and into the greased bowl, smoothing the top with moistened fingers or a rubber spatula dipped in water. Cover the bowl loosely with a sheet of oiled plastic wrap or a damp tea towel and place it in a warm, draft-free spot. Allow the dough to rise for 2 hours, or until it has doubled in bulk.

Preheat the oven to 500°F/260°C with a pizza stone on the middle rack. Cover a baking sheet with parchment paper or a silicone baking mat.

Punch down the dough. Divide the dough in half and form each half into a ball, rolling it in brown rice flour to keep it from being sticky. Place 1 ball of dough on the prepared baking sheet, dust the baking sheet with rice flour, and, with a rolling pin dusted with rice flour, form the dough into a 12-inch/30.5 cm circle.

Top the pizza crust with your favorite toppings. Set the baking sheet on top of the preheated pizza stone and bake it for 12 to 15 minutes, or until the topping is bubbly and the crust is browned and crisp. Serve immediately. Repeat with the remaining dough for a second pizza.

NOTE:

The dough balls can be refrigerated for up to 3 days, tightly wrapped in plastic wrap.

VARIATIONS:

- Add 2 tablespoons/4.25 g of chopped fresh herbs (some combination of oregano, basil, thyme, and rosemary) to the dough.
- Add 2 tablespoons/17 g of crushed roasted garlic to the dough.
- Add ½ cup/40 g of freshly grated Parmesan cheese to the dough.

The first documented use of the word *pizza* was in 997 CE in the southern Italian town of Gaeta, and at that time meant a cross between what we today call lavash and focaccia. By the late nineteenth century, pizza was the staple street food of Naples, sold at breakfast, lunch, and dinner. From there it came to the United States with the large wave of immigration from southern Italy and Sicily.

Lavash

LAVASH IS ONE OF THE OLDEST FLATBREADS that is still a dietary staple in its birthplace—in this case, Armenia. But it is a versatile bread, to be sure, because its texture ranges from soft and pliable to crisp and crackerlike, depending on how long it's baked. I use lavash a lot for wrap sandwiches because it comes in a rectangle, which makes the sandwiches even and neat.

MAKES ONE 15 × 10-INCH/38 × 25.5 CM SHEET

2 tablespoons/30 g ground chia seeds
1 tablespoon/12 g active dry yeast
2 teaspoons/8 g granulated sugar
¾ cup/178 ml water, heated to 110° to 115°F/43° to 46°C
½ cup/64 g sorghum flour
¼ cup/30 g teff flour
¼ cup/42.5 g potato starch
¼ cup/31 g tapioca flour
¼ cup/17 g nonfat dried milk powder
1¼ teaspoons/11.25 g xanthan gum
¾ teaspoon/4.5 g fine salt
2 tablespoons/30 ml olive oil

Combine the chia seeds, yeast, sugar, and water in the bowl of a stand mixer fitted with the paddle attachment and mix well. Set aside for about 10 minutes while the yeast proofs. Combine the sorghum flour, teff flour, potato starch, tapioca flour, milk powder, xanthan gum, and salt in a deep mixing bowl and whisk well.

When the yeast looks frothy add the olive oil and mix well. Add the dry ingredients and beat at medium speed until combined. Increase the speed to high and beat the dough for 3 to 5 minutes, or until it has the consistency of a thick cake batter that would require spreading in a cake pan; it is too thick to pour.

(recipe continues)

Lightly grease the inside of a large mixing bowl with vegetable oil or softened butter. Scrape the dough out of the mixer bowl and into the greased bowl, smoothing the top with moistened fingers or a rubber spatula dipped in water. Cover the bowl loosely with a sheet of oiled plastic wrap or a damp tea towel and place it in a warm, draft-free spot. Allow the dough to rise for 1 hour, or until it has doubled in bulk.

Preheat the oven to 400°F/200°C. Cut a sheet of parchment paper to fit the bottom of a 15 × 10-inch/38 × 25.5 cm rimmed baking sheet and grease the sides of the pan.

Punch down the dough and spread the dough evenly in the prepared pan, using a rubber spatula dipped in water or your wet hands. The dough will be very thin. Bake the bread in the center of the oven for 12 to 15 minutes, or until the edges are brown and the center is firm. Allow the bread to cool completely in the pan before removing and storing it.

NOTE:

The bread is best the day it is baked, but it can be stored refrigerated, tightly covered with plastic wrap, for up to 2 days.

VARIATIONS:

- Add 1 tablespoon/3 g of herbes de Provence to the dough.
- Add 3 tablespoons/25.5 g of mashed roasted garlic to the dough.

Lavash is eaten all through the Caucasus, as well as in Iran, Lebanon, and Syria. It is traditionally baked in a tandoor-style oven called a *tonir*. Armenians would bake lavash for the winter in the fall, after the wheat harvest, and store it dried. They would moisten it to make it supple again before eating it.

Socca

SOCCA, MADE WITH GARBANZO BEAN FLOUR, is a street food unique to Nice and the rest of France's sun-drenched Côte d'Azur. The first time I toured a market in Nice, an aroma wafting along the street was a combination of garlic, rosemary, and some sort of bread. It turned out to be socca, and I've been hooked ever since. It comes out a medium brown color, and I serve it with any Provençal specialty, such as bouillabaisse.

SERVES 4 TO 6

1 cup/120 g garbanzo bean flour
½ teaspoon/3 g fine salt
¾ teaspoon/1.5 g freshly ground black pepper
1 cup/237 ml lukewarm water
2 tablespoons/4.5 g chopped fresh rosemary, divided
5 tablespoons/75 ml olive oil, divided
2 garlic cloves, finely minced

Combine the garbanzo bean flour, salt, and pepper in a mixing bowl. Slowly whisk in the water until smooth. Whisk in 1 tablespoon/2.25 g of the rosemary, 2 tablespoons/30 ml of the olive oil, and the garlic. Allow the batter to sit for at least 2 hours.

Place one oven rack in the broiler position and place the other one in the center of the oven. Preheat the oven to 450°F/230°C. During the last 10 minutes of preheating, place a 12-inch/30.5 cm ovenproof skillet in the oven. Add 2 tablespoons/30 ml of the oil to the skillet and tilt to cover it evenly. Add the batter and bake for 12 to 15 minutes, or until the edges of the pancake are set.

(recipe continues)

Remove the skillet from the oven and preheat the oven broiler. Broil the bread 6 inches/15 cm from the broiler element for 2 to 3 minutes, or until firm and brown spots appear. Brush the bread with the remaining 3 tablespoons/45 ml of oil, sprinkle with the remaining 1 tablespoon/2.25 g of the rosemary, and serve hot.

NOTE:

The batter can sit at room temperature for up to 12 hours. Do not cook the bread until just prior to serving.

VARIATIONS:

- Substitute shallots for the garlic.
- Substitute a combination of oregano, basil, and thyme for the rosemary.

Chapatis

ON THE INDIAN SUBCONTINENT, chapati is the equivalent of a flour tortilla: It's cooked dry on a hot griddle after being rolled out thinly. But unlike flour tortillas, chapatis contain some seasoning so they have a flavor of their own, as well as functioning as a combination plate and fork. If you have a tortilla press, use it for chapatis, too. It will save you the time of rolling out all the balls of dough.

MAKES 12 CHAPATIS

- 2 cups/240 g garbanzo bean flour, plus more for rolling
- ¼ cup/32 g cornstarch
- 1½ teaspoons/3 g cumin seeds
- ½ teaspoon/3 g fine salt
- Freshly ground black pepper
- 2 tablespoons/30 ml olive oil
- ⅔ cup/158 ml water, heated to 140° to 150°F/60° to 65°C

Combine the 2 cups/240 g of garbanzo bean flour and the cornstarch, cumin seeds, salt, and pepper in a mixing bowl. Whisk well. Stir the oil into the hot water and pour the mixture slowly over the dry ingredients. Stir with a wooden spoon until the mixture becomes a sticky dough.

Dust a counter heavily with garbanzo bean flour. Place the dough on the counter and knead it for 2 minutes, or until it comes together as a mass. Work in more garbanzo bean flour if the dough is too sticky and drizzle with additional water if it is too dry. Divide the dough into twelve equal parts and roll each part into a ball.

Flatten 1 ball into a disk in the palm of your hand. Dust the disk with garbanzo bean flour and use a rolling pin dusted with flour to form a 7-inch/18 cm round, rolling from the center outward in all directions. Roll the remaining dough in the same fashion, stacking them with sheets of waxed paper between them.

Heat a 12-inch/30.5 cm nonstick skillet over medium-high heat for at least 3 minutes. Place 1 chapati in the pan and cook for 1½ minutes, or until bubbles appear on the surface. Turn over the chapati gently with a spatula and cook for an additional 45 seconds to 1 minute. Repeat with the remaining dough rounds, and serve hot.

NOTE:

The chapatis can be rolled and stacked up to a day in advance and refrigerated. Do not cook them until just prior to serving because they become brittle once they cool.

Naan

THERE'S NO QUESTION that naan is my favorite flatbread. First of all, it has a lighter texture than most flatbreads, and it contains butter. That's always a plus for me. The great news is that you really don't need a tandoor oven to make delicious naan. It's true that when using a cast-iron skillet, you don't have the experience of slapping up hunks of dough onto the hot stone walls of the oven. But you also don't risk burning your hands on the stone walls of a hot oven.

MAKES 8 NAAN

1½ teaspoons/6 g active dry yeast
2 teaspoons/8 g granulated sugar
½ cup/118 ml water, heated to 110° to 115°F/43° to 46°C
1½ cups/237 g brown rice flour, plus more for rolling
½ cup/85 g potato starch
½ cup/62.5 g tapioca flour
⅓ cup/68 g sweet rice flour
¼ teaspoon/1 g gluten-free baking powder
1½ teaspoons/4.5 g xanthan gum
½ teaspoon/3 g fine salt
2 large eggs, at room temperature
⅔ cup/152 g unsalted butter, melted and cooled, divided
¼ cup/59 ml plain nonfat yogurt

Combine the yeast, sugar, water, and ¼ cup/40 g of the brown rice flour in the bowl of a stand mixer fitted with the paddle attachment and mix well. Set aside for about 10 minutes while the yeast proofs. Combine the brown rice flour, potato starch, tapioca flour, sweet rice flour, baking powder, xanthan gum, and salt in a deep mixing bowl and whisk well.

(recipe continues)

When the yeast looks frothy add the eggs, ⅓ cup/75 g of the melted butter, and the yogurt. Add the dry ingredients and beat at medium speed until combined. Increase the speed to high and beat the dough for 3 to 5 minutes, or until the dough has the consistency of a thick cake batter that would require spreading in a cake pan; it is too thick to pour.

Lightly grease the inside of a large mixing bowl with olive oil or butter. Scrape the dough out of the mixer bowl and into the greased bowl, smoothing the top with moistened fingers or a rubber spatula dipped in water. Cover the bowl loosely with a sheet of oiled plastic wrap or a damp tea towel and place it in a warm, draft-free spot. Allow the dough to rise for 1 to 2 hours, or until it has doubled in bulk.

Have a bowl of additional brown rice flour and a bowl of tepid water on the counter. Punch down the dough and divide it into 8 parts; the dough will be sticky. Roll each ball in the rice flour as you divide it, and sprinkle flour on your counter, too.

Roll out each ball into a 7-inch/18 cm circle.

Heat a large skillet over high heat for at least 3 minutes, or until it is almost smoking. Dampen your hands in the water bowl and rub both sides of a piece of naan to lightly dampen it. Place the dampened piece of dough in the skillet and cook for 1 minute, or until the dough starts to bubble. Turn the bread with tongs, cover the skillet, and cook for 45 seconds to 1 minute, or until the bottom is browned. Remove the naan from the skillet and brush both sides with the remaining melted butter. Repeat with the remaining dough balls. Serve hot.

NOTE:

The breads can be cooked up to 3 hours in advance and kept at room temperature. Before serving, reheat them in a skillet placed over medium heat.

The first recorded history of naan can be found in the notes of the Indo-Persian poet Amir Khusrau in 1300 CE. From around 1526, during the Mughal era in India, naan accompanied by kebabs was a popular breakfast food of the royals.

Naan is traditionally cooked in a tandoor, or clay oven, and it's yeasted, unlike chapati and other flatbreads commonly referred to as roti. In India, naan is cooked in a teardrop shape, while in most other places in South Asia it's round. The Burmese version resembles a puffed pita bread but is still called naan.

Corn Tortillas

CORN TORTILLAS ARE AS TRADITIONAL to Mexican cooking as baguettes are to French. They go stale even more quickly and should be eaten as soon as they're cooked.

The ingredients for fresh tortillas are simple: masa harina, a corn flour that is treated with calcium hydroxide to release the niacin in the corn and to make it easier on digestion, and water. These two ingredients, along with a touch of salt, are combined into dough and are then either rolled out by hand or pressed with a tortilla press and cooked over high heat on a griddle.

MAKES 16 TORTILLAS

1¾ cups/217 g masa harina

¾ teaspoon/4.5 g fine salt

1 cup/237 ml plus 2 tablespoons/30 ml water, heated to 140° to 150°F/60° to 65°C

Combine the masa harina, salt, and water in a mixing bowl and stir well until the mixture is combined. Sprinkle additional masa harina on a counter and knead the dough for 2 to 3 minutes, or until smooth and pliable. Add a bit more masa harina if the dough is sticky and add a bit more water if it begins to dry out. Wrap the dough tightly in plastic wrap and allow it to rest for at least 30 minutes.

Divide the dough into 16 parts and roll each part into a ball. Place 1 ball between 2 sheets of plastic wrap and flatten it to an even thickness of ⅓ inch/0.8 cm, using a tortilla press or rolling pin. Preheat a 12-inch/30.5 cm skillet or griddle over medium-high heat while pressing or rolling the remaining balls of dough.

Place a tortilla in the pan and cook for 30 seconds, or until browned and starting to puff. Turn the tortilla gently with tongs and cook for another 30 seconds. Transfer the tortilla to a warmed plate and cover it with a damp towel to stay moist while cooking the remaining tortillas. Repeat with the remaining tortillas.

NOTE:

The tortillas can be prepared for cooking up to 1 day in advance and refrigerated between the sheets of plastic wrap. Do not cook them until just prior to serving to have the best texture.

HOMEMADE TORTILLA STRIPS

If you have any corn tortillas left over, turn them into baked tortilla chips. Preheat the oven to 400°F/200°C and cover a baking sheet with aluminum foil. With kitchen scissors, cut the tortillas into triangles and arrange them on the prepared baking sheet with at least ½ inch/1.25 cm of space between them. Mist them lightly with vegetable oil spray, sprinkle them with salt, and bake them for 10 to 12 minutes, or until browned and crispy (start checking them after 8 minutes). Allow them to cool for 10 minutes, then serve. You can also sprinkle them with herbs and spices or freshly grated Parmesan cheese before baking them.

Arepas

AREPAS ARE A STAPLE FOOD in both Venezuela and Colombia. They are corn cakes and related to tortillas, but they are made from a special precooked corn flour called *masarepa* that gives them the texture of a bread. In terms of both shape and consistency, they are sort of a hybrid between a tortilla and an English muffin. These simple, satisfying corn cakes are delicious with butter or cream cheese for breakfast, or as an accompaniment to any meal. Colombian arepas tend to be thinner than Venezuelan ones. The thicker ones are perfect for splitting and filling with cheese or meat.

MAKES 6 AREPAS

1 cup/160 g masarepa
½ teaspoon/3 g fine salt
1 cup/237 ml plus 2 tablespoons/30 ml water, heated to 140° to 150°F/60° to 65°C
1 cup/112 g grated whole-milk mozzarella
2 to 3 tablespoons/30 to 45 ml olive oil

Preheat the oven to 350°F/175°C and line a baking sheet with heavy-duty aluminum foil.

Combine the masarepa and salt in a mixing bowl. Make a well in the center and slowly stir in the water. When the dough comes together, stir in the cheese.

Transfer the dough to a counter sprinkled with additional masarepa and knead it for 5 minutes. Divide the dough into 6 pieces and form each into a ball. Flatten the balls into disks 3 inches/6 cm in diameter. Smooth the edges of the disks with the side of your hand.

(recipe continues)

Heat a large nonstick skillet over medium heat. Add the oil and tilt the pan to coat it evenly. Cook the arepas over medium-low heat for 6 to 7 minutes per side, or until very lightly browned. Transfer the arepas to the baking sheet and bake them for 15 to 20 minutes, or until they sound hollow when tapped. Remove the arepas from the oven and allow them to cool for 5 minutes.

NOTE:

The disks can be wrapped tightly in plastic wrap and refrigerated for up to 2 days.

Masarepa is precooked, ground corn flour that is used to prepare arepas. Arepas were traditionally made by soaking the corn and then manually pounding the grains to remove the seed germ and the outer lining. The remaining part of the corn was then cooked and ground and made into arepas. This labor-intensive process is now done on an industrial level, so you can buy the dried, precooked corn flour and make arepas quickly and easily. Masarepa should not be confused with masa harina, which is ground corn that has been treated with lime, used for making tortillas. Masarepa is available in the Latin American cooking section of most supermarkets, produced by such major brands as Goya and P.A.N. It's sometimes known as *masa al instante* and *harina precocida*.

Injeras with Caraway Seeds

WHEN I LIVED IN WASHINGTON, DC, my theory was that sooner or later the ambassador from every country would have a brother or cousin who wanted to open a restaurant featuring the native cuisine of their homeland. One then-hip, now-established part of the city called Adams Morgan was famous for its ethnic enclaves, including a number of Ethiopian restaurants. I grew really fond of ripping off a piece of injera to use as a fork, and even if you don't want to serve Ethiopian food, these make wonderful alternatives to crêpes for a savory meal.

MAKES 8 TO 10 INJERAS

1½ cups/180 g teff flour
2 cups/500 ml distilled water
½ teaspoon/3 g fine salt, or to taste
1½ teaspoons/3.3 g caraway seeds, crushed
Freshly ground black pepper to taste
2 to 3 tablespoons/30 to 45 ml olive oil

Combine the teff flour and distilled water in a large mixing bowl. Stir well. Cover the bowl with a damp tea towel and allow it to ferment for 2 to 3 days in a warm, draft-free place. It should be very bubbly and have grown in volume substantially.

Stir in the salt, caraway seeds, and pepper. The mixture will deflate and look like a thin pancake batter.

Heat an 8-inch/20 cm skillet over medium heat. Brush the skillet with olive oil and pour ¼ cup/30 g of the teff batter into the center of the skillet. Spread the batter by rotating the skillet in the air in a circular motion. Cook the injera for 2 to 3 minutes, or until holes form in the top, the top is dry, and the cooked edges lift from the sides of the pan. Do not flip the injera to cook the second side.

(recipe continues)

Remove the injera from the skillet with tongs and transfer it to a heated plate. Cook the remaining injeras in the same fashion, separating the cooked pancakes with layers of parchment paper. To serve, place a pancake on a dinner plate and top with your choice of stews. Serve extra injeras to use as utensils.

NOTE:

Once fermented, the batter can be refrigerated for up to 2 days, tightly covered with plastic wrap. Do not cook the injeras until just prior to serving.

VARIATION:

- Substitute cumin seeds or fennel seeds for the caraway seeds.

If you have an Active Sourdough Starter (page 49) living in your refrigerator, you can speed up the fermentation for this batter. Add a lump about the size of a walnut to the teff mixture and within 1 day it should have fermented enough to cook the injeras.

CHAPTER 5

Quick Breads

Rarely has a category of foods been so aptly named. Baking a quick bread necessitates no time for yeast to ferment and create gas bubbles. Chemical leavening agents create those necessary little balloons of carbon dioxide in the dough. And whether the quick bread is made gluten-free or with wheat flour, the dough has a soft consistency and is always baked in a loaf pan.

Quick breads are an American invention that began around the time of the Civil War when a lot of food was needed quickly and, as was the case later in World War II, many women who would watch their loaves rise had duties outside of the house while the menfolk were away.

You will find that the method of making gluten-free quick breads departs from the norm. When making these treats with wheat flour, you are always admonished to not over-mix the dough, so as to retard gluten formation. Well, without gluten, you can beat them for as long as you want, and the results are wonderful.

Quick breads can be sweet or savory, and they're extremely versatile because the same dough can be transformed into muffins by changing the baking temperature and time. You'll see that most of the recipes in this chapter bake at 350°F/175°C for just slightly less than an hour. If you want to make standard muffins, increase the temperature to 400°F/200°C and bake them for 18 to 22 minutes, and oversized muffins bake at 375°F/190°C for 20 to 25 minutes.

Because of the high moisture content of quick breads, they are very difficult to slice thinly. If you want to slice them thinly, the best thing to do is to refrigerate them well first. Quick breads are some of the most successful breads to freeze, for the same reason: the high moisture content. Wrap the slices individually and then stack them in a heavy resealable plastic bag, to enjoy them for up to three months.

THE DIFFERENCE BETWEEN BAKING POWDER AND BAKING SODA

When I was working as the food editor of a daily newspaper back in the 1970s, the phone rang constantly with questions from readers, most of which had absolutely nothing to do with any article I'd written. Remember, this was before Google.

One of the questions asked most often was the difference between baking soda and baking powder and whether one can be substituted for the other. They are both white powders that make foods rise as they bake. Readers would be curious as to why some recipes called for one or the other, and frequently recipes called for both. Here is a summary of what I'd tell them:

Baking soda is also known by its official name, sodium bicarbonate. When heated, this chemical compound forms carbon dioxide gas, which makes your quick breads rise. But here's the problem. That's not all it produces.

When heated, sodium bicarbonate also produces sodium carbonate, which has a nasty and unpleasant alkaline flavor. But if you mix baking soda with an acid, such as lemon juice or buttermilk, then the sodium carbonate is partially neutralized and leaves behind less of an aftertaste. This acid also helps the carbon dioxide gas release more quickly.

Baking powder is basically just baking soda with an acid already added, so there doesn't have to be one elsewhere in the recipe. It has just enough acid to use up the sodium carbonate. Food chemist Shirley Corriher, whom I've called many times over the years for guidance, says in her wonderful book *Cookwise* that 1 teaspoon/4.6 g of baking powder contains ¼ teaspoon/1.15 g of baking soda. The other ¾ teaspoon/3.45 g contains the acid—and cornstarch. A few companies use wheat-related products rather than cornstarch to cut the baking soda. That's why it's important to make sure that the baking powder you're using is gluten-free. The first commercial baking powder was made by the Rumford Chemical Works in Providence, Rhode Island, which still produces the powder, and is one of the companies that certifies it as gluten-free.

Because baking soda is four times as powerful as baking powder, use only ¼ teaspoon/1.15 g of baking soda for each teaspoon/4.6 g of baking powder if making a substitution for the latter in a recipe.

Baking powder does not last forever, even if you live in a dry climate. If you haven't used it in a few months, it's best to test it. Stir some into cold tap water. If it bubbles furiously, it's good to go. If you get just a modest fizz out of it, sort of like a can of almost flat soda, it's time to buy a new can.

Multiseed Bread

A COMBINATION OF NUTRITIOUS SEEDS provide a lot of texture in this bread, but the flavor remains very subtle and can be enjoyed at any time of day. This is a nice accompaniment to an elegant dinner, but it can also be used toasted and served with slices of cheese for a snack.

MAKES 1 LOAF

2 tablespoons/30 g ground chia seeds
½ cup/118 ml buttermilk, shaken
½ cup/60 g garbanzo bean flour
⅔ cup/85 g cornstarch
⅔ cup/83 g tapioca flour
3 tablespoons/24 g sorghum flour
2 tablespoons/15 g teff flour
2 tablespoons/28 g firmly packed dark brown sugar
1 teaspoon/2 g unflavored gelatin or agar powder
2 teaspoons/8 g gluten-free baking powder
1½ teaspoons/6 g baking soda
½ teaspoon/3 g fine salt
3 large eggs, at room temperature
4 tablespoons (½ stick)/56 g unsalted butter, melted and cooled
1 tablespoon/15 ml honey
1 tablespoon/8 g toasted sesame seeds
1 tablespoon/10 g flaxseeds
½ cup/80 g toasted pumpkin seeds
½ cup/62 g sunflower seeds

Preheat the oven to 350°F/175°C and grease a 9 × 5-inch/23 × 11 cm loaf pan with vegetable oil spray. Stir the chia seeds into the buttermilk and set aside for 10 minutes.

Combine the garbanzo bean flour, cornstarch, tapioca flour, sorghum flour, teff flour, brown sugar, gelatin, baking powder, baking soda, and salt in a large, deep

(recipe continues)

mixing bowl and whisk well. Whisk together the eggs, melted butter, honey, and chia seed mixture in another bowl. Add the wet ingredients to the dry ingredients. Stir well. Stir in the sesame seeds and flaxseeds.

Scrape the dough into the prepared pan and smooth the top with a rubber spatula dipped in water. Sprinkle the pumpkin seeds and sunflower seeds evenly on top of the loaf.

Bake the bread for 55 to 60 minutes, or until a toothpick inserted into the center comes out clean. Check the bread after 30 minutes and cover it loosely with aluminum foil if it is getting too brown. Place the pan on a cooling rack and let cool for 30 minutes, then turn the bread out of the pan and serve.

NOTE:

The bread can be served hot or at room temperature. Once cool, keep it refrigerated, tightly wrapped in plastic wrap, for up to 2 days.

VARIATION:

- Substitute caraway seeds for the sesame seeds to create a mock rye bread flavor.

Irish Soda Bread with Currants and Caraway Seeds

ALTHOUGH CELEBRATING St. Patrick's Day by feasting on corned beef and cabbage is not an authentic Irish tradition, soda bread is an important part of that island's cuisine. Soda bread as we know it today came into being in the late-nineteenth century with the introduction of baking soda, and its traditional forms are both dark and light. Zesty dried currants and aromatic caraway seeds punctuate this version.

MAKES 2 LOAVES

2½ cups/395 g brown rice flour, plus more for dusting the pans
½ cup/118 ml freshly squeezed orange juice
⅔ cup/96 g dried currants
⅔ cup/113 g potato starch
½ cup/62.5 g tapioca flour
2 tablespoons/25 g granulated sugar
1½ teaspoons/6 g baking soda
1 teaspoon/9 g xanthan gum
½ teaspoon/3 g fine salt
1¾ cups/425 ml buttermilk, shaken
6 tablespoons (¾ stick)/83 g unsalted butter, melted and cooled, divided
2 tablespoons/13 g caraway seeds

Preheat the oven to 375°F/190°C, grease two 8-inch/20 cm round cake pans, and dust them with rice flour. Bring the orange juice to a boil in a small saucepan or microwave-safe bowl. Add the currants and allow them to soak for 15 minutes, or until needed.

Combine the 2½ cups/395 g of rice flour and the potato starch, tapioca flour, sugar, baking soda, xanthan gum, and salt in a deep mixing bowl and whisk well. Add the buttermilk and ¼ cup/56 g of the melted butter and stir well for 2 minutes with a

(recipe continues)

wooden spoon. Drain the currants, discarding any remaining orange juice, and stir the currants and caraway seeds into the dough.

Divide the dough in half and pat each half into a 6-inch/15 cm round in the center of a prepared pan. Cut a ½-inch/1.25 cm-deep X on top of each round and brush the tops with the remaining 2 tablespoons/27 g of melted butter.

Bake the breads for 35 to 40 minutes, or until the tops are golden brown. Allow the breads to cool in the pans for 20 minutes, then transfer them to a cooling rack and let cool for at least 10 minutes before slicing.

NOTE:

The bread can be served the day it is made, but it slices more easily if kept refrigerated, wrapped in plastic wrap, for 1 day.

VARIATION:

- Omit the currants and raisins and add ¾ cup/75 g of chopped scallions (white parts and 4 inches/8 cm of the green tops) to the dough.

Herbed Beer Bread

I NEVER THOUGHT IT WAS POSSIBLE to make gluten-free beer bread because almost all beer is made from malted barley, but there are now some on the market, such as Redbridge and Bard's, that are brewed from approved grains, such as sorghum. Beer produces the same yeasty smelling loaf as a raised bread, but in a fraction of the time. I particularly like the way that the subtle yeast flavor blends with those of the aromatic fresh herbs. This is a great bread to use in a strata recipe for a brunch, with some heady cheeses and crumbled sausage added to it, or as the basis for a poultry stuffing (page 67).

MAKES 1 LOAF

1¼ cups/159 g sorghum flour
1 cup/158 g brown rice flour
½ cup/64 g cornstarch
¼ cup/31 g tapioca flour
¼ cup/30 g teff flour
1 teaspoon/2 g unflavored gelatin or agar powder
1 teaspoon/4 g gluten-free baking powder
1 teaspoon/9 g xanthan gum
½ teaspoon/3 g fine salt
½ teaspoon/2 g baking soda
1 large egg, lightly beaten
1 (12-ounce/355 ml) can gluten-free lager beer
2 tablespoons/7.5 g chopped fresh parsley
1 tablespoon/2 g chopped fresh rosemary (substitute 1 teaspoon/1 g dried)
2 teaspoons/1.5 g fresh thyme (substitute ½ teaspoon/0.7 g dried)

Preheat the oven to 350°F/175°C and grease a 9 × 5-inch/23 × 11 cm loaf pan with vegetable oil spray.

Combine the sorghum flour, brown rice flour, cornstarch, tapioca flour, teff flour, gelatin, baking powder, xanthan gum, salt, and baking soda in a large, deep mixing bowl and whisk well. Whisk together the egg, beer, parsley, rosemary, and thyme. Add the wet mixture to the dry ingredients and stir well.

Scrape the dough into the prepared pan and smooth the top with a rubber spatula dipped in water.

Bake the bread for 45 to 55 minutes, or until a toothpick inserted into the center comes out clean. Check the bread after 30 minutes and cover it loosely with aluminum foil if it is getting too brown. Place the pan on a cooling rack and let cool for 30 minutes, then turn the bread out of the pan and serve.

NOTE:

The bread can be served hot or at room temperature. Once cool, keep it refrigerated, tightly wrapped in plastic wrap, for up to 2 days.

VARIATIONS:

- For a sweet version of this bread, omit the herbs and add ½ cup/106 g of firmly packed light brown sugar to the dough.
- Add ¼ cup/36 g of chopped kalamata olives and ¼ cup/13.5 g of chopped sun-dried tomatoes to the dough.

If you want to keep fresh herbs fresher for longer, trim the stems when you bring them home. Then place them in a glass of water, as if a bouquet of flowers, and refrigerate them. The water will double their life. You can also strip the herb leaves off dill and parsley and freeze small bundles wrapped in plastic wrap. When ready to use them, hit the bundles with the dull side of a knife to "chop" the herbs.

Sun-Dried Tomato and Olive Bread

IF YOU'RE HAVING a simple broiled or grilled entrée, then this aromatic and flavorful bread can become the star of the meal. Bits of salty olives and succulent sun-dried tomatoes dot every slice. Also try using it for grilled cheese sandwiches made with a combination of aged provolone or a combination of fresh mozzarella and smoked Gouda.

MAKES 1 LOAF

¾ cup/118.5 g brown rice flour
½ cup/64 g sorghum flour
½ cup/85 g potato starch
¼ cup/31 g tapioca flour
2 teaspoons/8 g gluten-free baking powder
1½ teaspoons/1 g Italian seasoning
1 teaspoon/9 g xanthan gum
½ teaspoon/2 g baking soda
½ teaspoon/3 g fine salt
Freshly ground black pepper as desired

2 large eggs, at room temperature
¾ cup/178 ml whole milk
½ cup/118 ml olive oil
½ cup/55 g finely chopped sun-dried tomatoes packed in olive oil, drained well
½ cup/67 g finely chopped oil-cured black olives
2 tablespoons/7.5 g chopped fresh parsley
2 garlic cloves, minced

Preheat the oven to 350°F/175°C and grease a 9 × 5-inch/23 × 11 cm loaf pan with vegetable oil spray.

Combine the rice flour, sorghum flour, potato starch, tapioca flour, baking powder, Italian seasoning, xanthan gum, baking soda, salt, and pepper in a deep,

(recipe continues)

large mixing bowl and whisk well. Whisk together the eggs, milk, and olive oil. Add the wet mixture to the dry ingredients and stir well. Stir in the tomatoes, olives, parsley, and garlic.

Scrape the dough into the prepared pan and smooth the top with a rubber spatula dipped in water.

Bake the bread for 40 to 45 minutes, or until a toothpick inserted into the center comes out clean. Check the bread after 30 minutes and cover it loosely with aluminum foil if it is getting too brown. Place the pan on a cooling rack and let cool for 30 minutes, then turn the bread out of the pan and serve.

NOTE:

The bread can be served hot or at room temperature. Once cool, keep it refrigerated, tightly wrapped in plastic wrap, for up to 2 days.

VARIATION:

- Substitute ⅔ cup/54 g of freshly grated Parmesan cheese for the sun-dried tomatoes and olives.

Always save the olive oil that surrounds the tomatoes in those pricey jars you buy. Use it in this recipe as part of the oil specified, but you can also use it in salad dressings. It has great flavor, and it's free. The reason to use sun-dried tomatoes packed in oil rather than those found loose is that those tomatoes really need to be soaked before they're added to a bread recipe, or else they will pull too much moisture out of the dough.

Butternut Squash Bread

ALL SORTS OF SWEET AND SAVORY dishes use puréed sweet potatoes as a base, but healthful winter squashes, such as butternut or acorn, are often overlooked as an ingredient for baked goods. Winter squash is the star of this quick bread. Its innate sweetness is magnified by the addition of a bit of brown sugar and spices, but this is essentially a savory loaf appropriate for any fall or winter meal.

MAKES 1 LOAF

¾ cup/87 g chopped walnuts
1 cup/140 g peeled, seeded, and diced butternut or acorn squash (about 5 ounces/142 g)
⅓ cup/42 g tapioca flour
⅓ cup/43 g cornstarch
⅓ cup/40 g garbanzo bean flour
2 tablespoons/16 g sorghum flour
1½ teaspoons/6 g gluten-free baking powder
1 teaspoon/2 g unflavored gelatin or agar powder
¼ teaspoon/0.5 g ground cinnamon
¼ teaspoon/0.5 g ground ginger
½ teaspoon/2 g baking soda
½ teaspoon/1.5 g xanthan gum
¼ teaspoon/1.5 g fine salt
4 tablespoons (½ stick)/56 g unsalted butter, at room temperature
½ cup/106 g firmly packed light brown sugar
1 large egg, at room temperature
½ cup/113 g small-curd cottage cheese

Preheat the oven to 350°F/175°C and grease an 8½ × 4½-inch/21.25 × 9.25 cm loaf pan with vegetable oil spray. Place the walnuts on a baking sheet and toast them for 5 to 7 minutes, or until browned. Set aside.

(recipe continues)

Cover the squash with salted water in a saucepan and bring to a boil over high heat. Lower the heat to medium and boil the squash, uncovered, for 10 to 15 minutes, or until very tender. Drain the squash, shaking it in a colander to rid it of as much water as possible, then purée it in a food processor fitted with the steel blade, or in a blender. Measure out ½ cup/118 ml of purée and reserve the remainder for another use.

Combine the tapioca flour, cornstarch, garbanzo bean flour, sorghum flour, baking powder, gelatin, cinnamon, ginger, baking soda, xanthan gum, and salt in a large, deep bowl and whisk well.

Combine the butter and brown sugar in the bowl of a stand mixer. Beat at low speed to combine, then raise the speed to high and beat for 3 to 5 minutes, or until light and fluffy. Scrape down the sides of the bowl as necessary. Add the egg, cottage cheese, and squash. Beat at medium speed until smooth. Add the dry ingredients at low speed and beat for 2 minutes. Stir in the walnuts.

Scrape the dough into the prepared pan and smooth the top with a rubber spatula dipped in water.

Bake the bread for 50 to 55 minutes, or until a toothpick inserted into the center comes out clean. Check the bread after 30 minutes and cover it loosely with aluminum foil if it is getting too brown. Place the pan on a cooling rack and let cool for 30 minutes, then turn the bread out of the pan and serve.

NOTE:

The bread can be served hot or at room temperature. Once cool, keep it refrigerated, tightly wrapped in plastic wrap, for up to 2 days.

VARIATION:

- Substitute ½ cup/58 g of canned solid-pack pumpkin for the squash.

Apricot Almond Bread

APRICOTS AND ALMONDS are members of the same botanic genus—*Prunus*—so it's not surprising that they taste so well together. In fact, in some Mediterranean countries, the pits from apricots are used as a substitute for almonds. This quick bread is simultaneously subtle and succulent. The combination of apricot nectar as well as dried apricots and almond meal as well as almonds reinforces the dominant flavors of the bread. This is a wonderful candidate to transform into a bread pudding because so much flavor emerges when the egg mixture is added.

MAKES 1 LOAF

½ cup/118 ml apricot nectar
1 cup/131 g finely chopped dried apricots
¾ cup/108 g chopped blanched almonds
½ cup/60 g garbanzo bean flour
½ cup/64 g cornstarch
½ cup/62.5 g tapioca flour
¼ cup/28 g almond meal
¼ cup/55 g firmly packed light brown sugar
2 teaspoons/8 g gluten-free baking powder
¾ teaspoon/6.75 g xanthan gum
½ teaspoon/2 g baking soda
½ teaspoon/3 g fine salt
2 large eggs, at room temperature
4 tablespoons (½ stick)/56 g unsalted butter, melted and cooled
½ teaspoon/2.5 ml pure almond extract

Preheat the oven to 350°F/175°C and grease a 9 × 5-inch/23 × 11 cm loaf pan with vegetable oil spray.

Bring the apricot nectar to a boil in a small saucepan and add the chopped dried apricots. Turn off the heat and allow the mixture to sit until needed. Place the almonds on a baking sheet and toast them for 5 to 7 minutes, or until browned. Set aside.

(recipe continues)

Combine the garbanzo bean flour, cornstarch, tapioca flour, almond meal, brown sugar, baking powder, xanthan gum, baking soda, and salt in a large mixing bowl and whisk well. Drain the chopped apricots, reserving the apricot nectar. Whisk together the nectar, eggs, melted butter, and almond extract. Add the wet mixture to the dry ingredients and stir well. Stir in the chopped apricots and almonds.

Scrape the dough into the prepared pan and smooth the top with a rubber spatula dipped in water.

Bake the bread for 50 to 55 minutes, or until a toothpick inserted into the center comes out clean. Check the bread after 30 minutes and cover it loosely with aluminum foil if it is getting too brown. Place the pan on a cooling rack and let cool for 30 minutes, then turn the bread out of the pan and serve.

NOTE:

The bread can be served hot or at room temperature. Once cool, keep it refrigerated, tightly wrapped in plastic wrap, for up to 2 days.

VARIATION:

- Substitute dried peaches and peach nectar for the apricots and apricot nectar, substitute chopped pecans for the almonds, and substitute pure vanilla extract for the almond extract.

Just ¼ cup/28 g of delicately flavored and versatile almonds contains almost half the vitamin E and manganese you need in the course of a day, and almonds are high in heart-healthy monounsaturated fat. For baking we frequently use blanched almonds, but the skin contains about twenty flavonoids similar to those found in green tea. Almonds are also high in protein.

Banana Bread

BANANA BREAD IS A CLASSIC go-to recipe when there are bananas getting overly ripe, which is when they have the best flavor. In my opinion, you should never eat a banana unless it is covered with dark spots. Bright yellow is not good enough. But it's a quick trip from "perfection" to "on the way out," which is where banana bread comes in. Crunchy pecans add some textural interest to this version, which is scented by rum as well as spices. Serve this aromatic bread for breakfast spread with cream cheese mixed with dried fruit, or topped with a hot fruit compote for dessert.

MAKES 1 LOAF

½ cup/54 g chopped pecans
½ cup/60 g millet flour
½ cup/79 g brown rice flour
½ cup/62.5 g tapioca flour
⅓ cup/43 g cornstarch
1½ teaspoons/6 g gluten-free baking powder
1 teaspoon/2 g unflavored gelatin or agar powder
¾ teaspoon/6.75 g xanthan gum
½ teaspoon/3 g fine salt
½ teaspoon/1 g ground cinnamon
Pinch of freshly grated nutmeg
12 tablespoons (1½ sticks)/165 g unsalted butter, at room temperature
½ cup/100 g granulated sugar
½ cup/110 g firmly packed dark brown sugar
1 large egg, at room temperature
1 cup very ripe mashed bananas (2 or 3, depending on size)
¼ cup/59 ml dark rum, or ½ teaspoon/2.5 ml rum extract mixed with ¼ cup/59 ml water
¼ cup/59 ml buttermilk, shaken
1 ripe banana, thinly sliced (optional)

(recipe continues)

Preheat the oven to 350°F/175°C and grease an 8½ × 4½-inch/21.25 × 9.25 cm loaf pan with vegetable oil spray. Place the pecans on a baking sheet and toast them for 5 to 7 minutes, or until browned.

Combine the millet flour, rice flour, tapioca flour, cornstarch, baking powder, gelatin, xanthan gum, salt, cinnamon, and nutmeg in a large, deep mixing bowl and whisk well.

Combine the butter, granulated sugar, and brown sugar in the bowl of a stand mixer. Beat at low speed to combine, then raise the speed to high and beat for 3 to 5 minutes, or until light and fluffy. Scrape down the sides of the bowl as necessary. Add the egg, mashed bananas, rum, and buttermilk. Beat at medium speed until smooth. Add the dry ingredients at low speed and beat for 2 minutes. Stir in the pecans.

Scrape the dough into the prepared pan and smooth the top with a rubber spatula dipped in water. Place overlapping slices of banana on top of the dough, if using.

Bake the bread for 50 to 55 minutes, or until a toothpick inserted into the center comes out clean. Check the bread after 30 minutes and cover it loosely with aluminum foil if it is getting too brown. Place the pan on a cooling rack and let cool for 30 minutes, then turn the bread out of the pan and serve.

NOTE:

The bread can be served hot or at room temperature. Once cool, keep it refrigerated, tightly wrapped in plastic wrap, for up to 2 days.

VARIATIONS:

- Substitute chopped dried apricots or raisins for the pecans.
- Substitute 2 tablespoons/21 g of finely chopped crystallized ginger for the cinnamon and nutmeg, and substitute ginger brandy for the rum.

If you have a number of bananas getting overly ripe, just put them into the freezer right in their peels. The peels will turn very black and dark, but they protect the flesh nicely. When you're ready to make banana bread or a smoothie, just let them thaw. It's much better for the banana to be frozen that way rather than as slices or a purée.

Very Berry Bread

THE GENRE OF QUICK BREADS contains lots of sweet as well as savory options. Just think of all those breakfast breads baked in a loaf pan. And this clearly fits into the former category. I've served this vividly colored and vibrantly flavored quick bread for dessert as well as at breakfast. Toast the slices and then top them with ice cream or sorbet. The combination of berry flavors is enhanced by the lemon in the dough.

MAKES 1 LOAF

1 cup/145 g fresh blueberries
1 cup/158 g brown rice flour
⅔ cup/113 g potato starch
¼ cup/31 g tapioca flour
1 tablespoon/12 g gluten-free baking powder
½ cup/100 g granulated sugar
1 teaspoon/2 g unflavored gelatin or agar powder
½ teaspoon/3 g fine salt
½ teaspoon/2 g baking soda
½ teaspoon/1.5 g xanthan gum
¾ cup/178 ml buttermilk, shaken
6 tablespoons (¾ stick)/83 g unsalted butter, melted and cooled
1 large egg, at room temperature
2 tablespoons/30 ml freshly squeezed lemon juice
1 teaspoon/2 g grated lemon zest
½ teaspoon/2.5 ml pure lemon extract
¾ cup/92 g fresh raspberries
¾ cup/108 g fresh blackberries

Preheat the oven to 350°F/175°C and grease a 9 × 5-inch/23 × 11 cm loaf pan with vegetable oil spray.

Place the blueberries in a food processor fitted with the steel blade and chop finely, using on-and-off pulsing. Set aside.

(*recipe continues*)

Combine the rice flour, potato starch, tapioca flour, baking powder, sugar, gelatin, salt, baking soda, and xanthan gum in a large, deep mixing bowl and whisk well. Whisk together the buttermilk, melted butter, egg, lemon juice, lemon zest, and lemon extract. Add the wet mixture to the dry ingredients and stir well. Stir in the chopped blueberries, raspberries, and blackberries.

Scrape the dough into the prepared pan and smooth the top with a rubber spatula dipped in water.

Bake the bread for 50 to 55 minutes, or until a toothpick inserted into the center comes out clean. Check the bread after 30 minutes and cover it loosely with aluminum foil if it is getting too brown. Place the pan on a cooling rack and let cool for 30 minutes, then turn the bread out of the pan and serve.

NOTE:

The bread can be served hot or at room temperature. Once cool, keep it refrigerated, tightly wrapped in plastic wrap, for up to 2 days.

Frozen fruit can be used in baking, but always use it in its frozen state. If you allow it to thaw, it will not measure correctly and will create too much liquid during baking. If using frozen fruit, the baking time will be in the upper end of the given range because it takes time for the chill of the frozen berries to be baked out of the dough.

Bacon and Cheese Cornbread

WHILE ALL AMERICAN REGIONAL CUISINES include some sort of cornbread (corn was the native crop), I tend to associate cornbread with the South and Southwest. This version is from that tradition, and cornbread doesn't get much heartier or vibrant than this version. The smoky, crunchy bacon serves as a perfect foil to the rich and mellow cheese. Serve this as part of a brunch with a dish of scrambled eggs and some baked tomatoes.

MAKES 1 LOAF

¼ pound/113 g bacon, diced
Vegetable oil, as necessary
½ cup/79 g brown rice flour
⅓ cup/57 g potato starch
3 tablespoons/23 g tapioca flour
1 cup/128 g finely ground yellow gluten-free cornmeal
1 tablespoon/12 g gluten-free baking powder
1 tablespoon/13 g granulated sugar
½ teaspoon/3 g fine salt
½ teaspoon/2 g baking soda
½ teaspoon/1.5 g xanthan gum
1 cup/237 ml buttermilk, shaken
1 large egg, at room temperature
1 cup/113 g grated Cheddar cheese, divided

Preheat the oven to 350°F/175°C and grease a 9 × 5-inch/23 × 11 cm loaf pan with vegetable oil spray.

Cook the bacon in a skillet over medium-high heat for 5 to 7 minutes, or until crisp. Remove the bacon from the pan with a slotted spoon and drain on paper towels. Set aside and crumble when cool. Pour the bacon grease into a cup and add vegetable oil as necessary to make ⅓ cup/79 ml.

(recipe continues)

Combine the rice flour, potato starch, tapioca flour, cornmeal, baking powder, sugar, salt, baking soda, and xanthan gum in a large, deep mixing bowl and whisk well. Whisk together the reserved bacon fat, buttermilk, and egg. Add the wet mixture to the dry ingredients and stir well. Stir in the bacon and ¾ cup/85 g of the cheese.

Scrape the dough into the prepared pan, smooth the top with a rubber spatula dipped in water, and sprinkle with the remaining ¼ cup/28 g of grated cheese.

Bake the bread for 45 to 50 minutes, or until a toothpick inserted into the center comes out clean. Check the bread after 30 minutes and cover it loosely with aluminum foil if it is getting too brown. Place the pan on a cooling rack and let cool for 30 minutes, then turn the bread out of the pan and serve.

NOTE:

The bread can be served hot or at room temperature. Once cool, keep it refrigerated, tightly wrapped in plastic wrap, for up to 2 days.

VARIATIONS:

- Substitute jalapeño Jack for the Cheddar, for a spicier bread.
- Add ¼ cup/65 g of finely chopped roasted red bell pepper to the dough.

If you don't want the bacon splattering over your stove, bake it on a rack over a rimmed baking sheet in a preheated 350°F/175°C oven until crisp. And if you have leftover bacon after making a recipe, roll up three or four slices, secure them with a toothpick, and freeze them in that configuration.

Pumpkin Cornbread with Roasted Corn

THE SPICED PUMPKIN is a great foil to the sweetness of the corn in this bread that is at home on a breakfast table or as part of a dinner. Michael Love, the specialty chef at Epicure Markets & Café in Miami, developed this bread as part of his upscale Epicure with Love line of products, and it was so good that I was determined to come up with a gluten-free version. It's really worth it to use fresh corn, even if it's out of season, for this recipe, rather than using frozen corn.

MAKES 1 LOAF

2 ears fresh corn (to yield 1 cup/164 g corn kernels)
1 cup/128 g finely ground yellow gluten-free cornmeal
¼ cup/30 g millet flour
¼ cup/31 g sorghum flour
¼ cup/32 g cornstarch
¼ cup/31 g tapioca flour
1 tablespoon/12 g gluten-free baking powder
1½ teaspoons/3 g curry powder
1 teaspoon/2.5 g ground cinnamon
1 teaspoon/2 g unflavored gelatin or agar powder
¼ teaspoon/½ g freshly grated nutmeg
½ teaspoon/3 g fine salt
2 large eggs, at room temperature
¾ cup/165 g firmly packed light brown sugar
½ cup/122 g canned solid-packed pure pumpkin (not pumpkin pie filling)
¼ cup/59 ml buttermilk, shaken
1 teaspoon/5 ml pure vanilla extract
6 tablespoons (¾ stick)/83 g unsalted butter, melted and cooled

Preheat the oven to 400°F/200°C and grease an 8½ × 4½-inch/21.25 × 9.25 cm loaf pan with vegetable oil spray.

Pull the husks down on the corn and remove the corn silks. Push the husks back over cobs and soak the ears in cold water for 5 minutes. Roast the corn on a baking sheet for 15 minutes. When cool enough to handle, cut the kernels from the cobs and set aside. Lower the oven temperature to 375°F/190°C.

Combine the cornmeal, millet flour, sorghum flour, cornstarch, tapioca flour, baking powder, curry powder, cinnamon, gelatin, nutmeg, and salt in a large, deep mixing bowl and whisk well. Whisk together the eggs, brown sugar, pumpkin, buttermilk, vanilla, and melted butter. Add the wet mixture to the dry ingredients and stir well. Stir in the corn kernels.

Scrape the dough into the prepared pan and smooth the top with a rubber spatula dipped in water.

Bake the bread for 45 to 50 minutes, or until a toothpick inserted into the center comes out clean. Check the bread after 30 minutes and cover it loosely with aluminum foil if it is getting too brown. Place the pan on a cooling rack to cool for 30 minutes, then turn the bread out of the pan and serve.

NOTE:

The bread can be served hot or at room temperature. Once cool, keep it refrigerated, tightly wrapped in plastic wrap for up to 2 days.

Be careful when purchasing cans of pumpkin, because the pure (solid-pack) purée is usually shelved right next to the pumpkin pie filling. The filling contains many other ingredients, such as spices and eggs, and, more important, it can also contain flour, so there's gluten in it.

Cornbread with Dried Fruit

CORNMEAL IS A VERY versatile grain. It takes well to assertive seasonings, such as chiles, and it also harmonizes beautifully with fruits to make a sweet confection. This lightly spiced version of cornbread, made with both dried cranberries and dried apricots, is a delicious morning sweet. But it can also be served alongside such entrées as roast poultry or pork. It's a pretty bread, too.

MAKES ONE 9-INCH/23 CM SQUARE PAN

1 cup/128 g finely ground yellow gluten-free cornmeal
⅔ cup/105 g brown rice flour
¼ cup/42.5 g potato starch
3 tablespoons/23 g tapioca flour
2 tablespoons/25 g granulated sugar
1½ teaspoons/6 g gluten-free baking powder
1 teaspoon/2 g unflavored gelatin or agar powder
1 teaspoon/9 g xanthan gum
½ teaspoon/2 g baking soda
¼ teaspoon/0.5 g ground cinnamon
¼ teaspoon/½ g freshly grated nutmeg
¼ teaspoon/1.5 g fine salt
2 large eggs, at room temperature
¾ cup/178 ml buttermilk, shaken
½ cup/128 g creamed corn
2 tablespoons/30 ml honey
5 tablespoons/71 g unsalted butter, melted and cooled
⅓ cup/36 g dried cranberries
⅓ cup/43 g finely chopped dried apricots

Preheat the oven to 425°F/218°C and grease a 9 × 9-inch/23 × 23 cm baking pan with vegetable oil spray.

Combine the cornmeal, rice flour, potato starch, tapioca flour, sugar, baking powder, gelatin, xanthan gum, baking soda, cinnamon, nutmeg, and salt in a deep mixing bowl and whisk well. Whisk together the eggs, buttermilk, creamed corn, honey,

(recipe continues)

and melted butter in a small bowl. Add the buttermilk mixture to the dry ingredients and stir well. Stir in the dried cranberries and dried apricots. Scrape the batter into the prepared pan.

Bake the cornbread in the middle of the oven for 15 minutes, or until the top is golden brown and the sides begin to pull away from the edges of the pan. Place the pan on a cooling rack and let cool for 30 minutes, then turn the bread out of the pan and serve.

NOTE:

The bread can be served hot or at room temperature. Once cool, keep it refrigerated, tightly wrapped in plastic wrap, for up to 2 days.

VARIATION:

- Substitute finely chopped dried pineapple and mango for the cranberries and apricots, and substitute ground ginger for the cinnamon and nutmeg.

CORNBREAD STUFFING WITH FRUIT

You already have a lot of fruit in the bread itself, so this is a natural to take to the next step to create a stuffing. I serve this fruited cornbread stuffing with both poultry and pork. While the fruit is succulent, the stuffing is not sweet.

SERVES 4 TO 6

6 tablespoons (¾ stick)/83 g unsalted butter
1 large onion, diced
2 celery ribs, diced
1 cup/237 ml chicken stock
2 Golden Delicious apples, peeled, cored, and diced
½ cup/66 g chopped dried apricots
¼ cup/31 g dried cranberries
2 tablespoons/7 g chopped fresh parsley
1 teaspoon/1 g fresh thyme leaves (substitute ½ teaspoon/0.75 g dried)
3 cups/221 g crumbled stale cornbread
Salt and freshly ground black pepper as desired

Preheat the oven to 350°F/175°C and grease a 13 × 9-inch/33 × 23-cm baking dish.

Heat the butter in a large, covered skillet over medium-high heat. Add the onion and celery and cook, stirring frequently, for 3 minutes, or until the onion is translucent. Add the stock, apples, dried apricots, dried cranberries, parsley, and thyme and bring to a boil, stirring occasionally. Lower the heat to low, cover the skillet, and simmer the mixture for 15 minutes, or until the vegetables are tender. Stir in the cornbread and season to taste with salt and pepper.

Transfer the stuffing to the prepared pan. Cover the pan with aluminum foil and bake for 30 minutes. Remove the foil and bake for an additional 10 minutes, or until the top is slightly crisp.

CHAPTER 6

Rolls

Up until this point, all of our breads have been large loaves. This chapter contains recipes for individual rolls to complement the slices of bread in your basket. Many of them are classics. They range from light and tender buttermilk biscuits and their first cousin, traditional English scones, to light and eggy popovers and dinner rolls like the ones Grandma would serve on a holiday. But then there are some more inventive options, made with such ingredients as cheese or sweet potatoes, too.

You'll notice that a few of the recipes contain both yeast and baking powder. I discovered that this double whammy of leavening agents gave them a more appealing crumb and texture and pushed them to rise faster during the relatively short bake time.

Although we may think of rolls as being a rather contemporary form of bread baking, they actually have a long and illustrious history. Individual rolls have been found in the tombs of ancient Egyptian pharaohs, and, by the Middle Ages, rolls were transformed into trenchers, which were a combination of plates and eating utensils.

In some respects, rolls are the next generation of flatbreads, the recipes for which can be found in Chapter 4. Like chapati or arepas, these rolls are made in individual pieces. But instead of being cooked individually, they are baked at the same time in the oven.

The chapter begins with yeasted rolls and then goes into the wonderful genre of biscuits and scones that rely on chemical leavening.

Old-Fashioned Dinner Rolls

THIS IS THE SORT of vaguely sweet roll tasting of eggs and butter that is always popular with everyone at the table, and has been part of many families' holiday traditions for generations. If you have a small cookie scoop or melon baller you can make three balls of dough in each of the muffin cups, for a pretty presentation. They don't remain the sort of distinct balls you'd have of ice cream, but they do hold some of the round shape.

MAKES 12 ROLLS

1 tablespoon/12 g active dry yeast
1 teaspoon/4 g granulated sugar
1 cup/237 ml whole milk, heated to 110° to 115°F/43° to 46°C, divided
1½ cups/239 g white rice flour
¼ cup/28 g defatted soy flour
⅓ cup/57 g potato starch
¼ cup/31 g tapioca flour
¼ cup/51 g sweet rice flour
3 tablespoons/12.75 g nonfat dried milk powder
1½ teaspoons/6 g gluten-free baking powder
1¼ teaspoons/11.25 g xanthan gum
½ teaspoon/3 g fine salt
2 large eggs, at room temperature, divided
3 tablespoons/42 g unsalted butter, melted and cooled
2 tablespoons/30 ml honey
1 teaspoon/5 ml distilled white vinegar

Grease a standard 12 cup muffin tin. Combine the yeast, sugar, and ½ cup/118 ml of the warm milk in the bowl of a stand mixer fitted with the paddle attachment and mix well. Set aside for about 10 minutes while the yeast proofs. Combine the white

(recipe continues)

rice flour, soy flour, potato starch, tapioca flour, sweet rice flour, milk powder, baking powder, xanthan gum, and salt in a deep mixing bowl and whisk well.

When the yeast looks frothy add the remaining ½ cup/118 ml of warm milk, 1 egg, and the melted butter, honey, and vinegar and mix well. Add the dry ingredients and beat at medium speed until combined. Increase the speed to high and beat the dough for 3 to 5 minutes, or until the dough has the consistency of a thick cake batter that would require spreading in a cake pan; it is too thick to pour.

Divide the dough into the prepared muffin tins. Cover the muffin tin with a sheet of oiled plastic wrap or a damp tea towel. Allow the rolls to rise in a warm place for 35 to 40 minutes, or until almost doubled in size. Beat the remaining egg and brush it gently over the tops of the rolls.

Preheat the oven to 375°F/190°C toward the end of the rising time.

Bake the rolls for 17 to 20 minutes, or until browned. Place the pan on a cooling rack and allow the rolls to cool for 20 minutes before serving.

NOTE:

The rolls are best the day they are baked, but they can be stored refrigerated, tightly covered with plastic wrap, for up to 2 days.

VARIATIONS:

- For sweeter rolls, increase the amount of honey to ⅓ cup/112 g.
- Sprinkle 2 tablespoons of sesame seeds or poppy seeds on the top of the rolls before baking.

When you're measuring viscous ingredients, such as honey or molasses, spray your measuring cup or measuring spoon with vegetable oil spray. The sticky liquid will slip right off. Otherwise you should use a rubber spatula to make a conscious effort to scrape all the liquid out of the measuring device, or else you won't have an accurate measure.

Bagels

IT'S TIME FOR TRUE CONFESSIONS: Until I started writing this book, I'd never made a bagel. I grew up in New York, where you can buy bagels on every block and then argue with your friends about which baker produces the *best* bagels. Rather than starting with gluten-free bagels, I eased into the process with bagels made with wheat flour. I tried many ways of forming them and tried all the methods of boiling them just risen or boiling them after they'd been baked for a few minutes in a hot oven. Once I felt confident about my methods, I then moved to gluten-free formulations and started the whole process again. Warning: This is a project for a whole day. But I will say by way of encouragement that I've tasted the gluten-free bagels on the market, and it's worth your whole day to make these. Fine smoked salmon deserves nothing less!

MAKES 6 BAGELS

Cornmeal, as needed
Vegetable shortening or vegetable oil
2 tablespoons/30 g ground chia seeds
4 teaspoons/16 g active dry yeast
⅓ cup/66.5 g granulated sugar, divided
1 cup/237 ml water, heated to 110° to 115°F/43° to 46°C
1 cup/158 g brown rice flour
1 cup/127 g sorghum flour
¾ cup/96 g cornstarch
¼ cup/42.5 g potato starch
2 tablespoons/14 g defatted soy flour
2 tablespoons/8.5 g nonfat dried milk powder
1½ teaspoons/4.5 g xanthan gum
½ teaspoon/3 g fine salt
2 large eggs, at room temperature
1 tablespoon/8 g poppy seeds, sesame seeds, or a combination, for topping (optional)
1 tablespoon/15 g kosher salt, for topping (optional)
1 shallot, minced and fried in 2 tablespoons/30 ml olive oil, for topping (optional)

(recipe continues)

Cover a baking sheet with parchment paper or a silicone baking mat and dust it with cornmeal. Grease another baking sheet thoroughly with vegetable shortening. Cut six 12 × 12-inch (30.5 × 30.5 cm) sheets of aluminum foil. Crush each sheet into a ball, then press the ball into a 2½-inch/6.25 cm-high × 1½-inch/3.75 cm-wide rectangular shape.

Combine the chia seeds, yeast, 1 tablespoon/13 g of the sugar, and ¾ cup/178 ml of the warm water in the bowl of a stand mixer fitted with the paddle attachment and mix well. Set aside for about 10 minutes while the yeast proofs. Combine the brown rice flour, sorghum flour, cornstarch, potato starch, soy flour, milk powder, xanthan gum, and salt in a deep mixing bowl and whisk well. Separate 1 of the eggs, setting aside the egg white.

When the yeast looks frothy add the remaining ¼ cup/59 ml of warm water, the remaining whole egg, and the egg yolk and mix well. Add the dry ingredients and beat at medium speed until combined. Increase the speed to high and beat the dough for 3 to 5 minutes, or until the dough holds together and has the consistency of a drop biscuit dough. Add more rice flour by 1 tablespoon/10 g amounts if necessary.

Grease your hands thoroughly with vegetable shortening or vegetable oil. Divide the dough into 6 parts and place them on the greased baking sheet. Use your hands to create a perfectly smooth ball from each portion of the dough and arrange them on the cornmeal-dusted baking sheet, spaced evenly apart. Pat down each ball to a 2-inch/5 cm-high disk. Create a hole in the middle of each disk with your index finger, moving it in ever-larger circles, then insert 1 of the foil plugs in each hole so that the 2½-inch/6.25 cm side sticks up above the bagel. Cover the bagels with a sheet of oiled plastic wrap and allow it to rise in a warm place for 45 to 60 minutes, or until the bagels have doubled in size.

Preheat the oven to 425°F/218°C toward the end of the rising time. Fill a deep skillet or Dutch oven with 6 inches/15 cm of water and add the remaining scant ⅓ cup/53.5 g sugar. Bring it to a boil over high heat.

Bake the bagels for 4 minutes, then remove them from the oven. Lower the oven temperature to 400°F/200°C.

The size of your bagels and the size of your pan will determine how many can be boiled simultaneously. Boil the bagels for 3 minutes per side, turning them gently with a slotted spatula. Allow them to drain for 5 minutes on a cooling rack set over a baking sheet or paper towels.

Beat the reserved egg white with 3 tablespoons/45 ml of water. Gently brush this mixture on the top of the bagels. Sprinkle the bagels with your desired topping, if using, patting it down very gently.

(recipe continues)

Bake the bagels for 20 to 25 minutes, or until golden brown. Allow the bagels to cool on a cooling rack for at least 30 minutes before slicing them.

NOTE:

The bagels are best the day they are baked, but they can be stored refrigerated, tightly covered with plastic wrap, for up to 2 days.

VARIATIONS:

- Add ¾ teaspoon/1.5 g of ground cinnamon to the dry ingredients and work ½ cup/72.5 g of raisins into the dough.
- Add ½ cup/56 g of grated sharp Cheddar or Gruyère cheese to the dough.
- Add ½ cup/78 g of thawed and well-drained chopped frozen spinach to the dough.

There are a few theories on the history of bagels, and this one is attributed to Leo Rosten, the author of *The Joys of Yiddish*, who spent many years researching food as part of his topic. He said that bagels are mentioned as early as 1610 in the city of Krakow, Poland, where they were given as gifts to women in childbirth. They became popular all over Eastern Europe by the time of the large Jewish immigration to New York in the late-nineteenth century, where they established a community. Bagels remained in primarily Jewish neighborhoods of the Northeast until the 1960s, when Harry Lender developed the process of mass production and shipped bagels frozen.

English Muffins

IF YOU LOVE THOSE NOOKS and crannies as much as I do, then it's worth the time to make your own English muffins. Like bagels, these rounds of griddled and then baked dough take some time, but the gluten-free version is no more labor intensive than are those made with wheat flour. The key to the perfect English muffin is to make them in an egg ring, and what I discovered was that cans of tuna were the same size. So if you're fond of tuna salad, remove the bottom of the tin as well as the top with the can opener, and you've got egg rings.

MAKES 8 MUFFINS

- 2 tablespoons/30 g ground chia seeds
- 2¼ teaspoons/7 g active dry yeast
- 2 teaspoons/10 ml honey
- 1¼ cups/300 ml buttermilk, heated to 110° to 115°F/43° to 46°C
- ¾ cup/90 ml millet flour
- ¾ cup/96 g cornstarch
- ¾ cup/94 g tapioca flour
- ½ cup/64 g sorghum flour
- ¼ cup/39 g brown rice flour, plus more for dusting
- ¼ cup/31 g masa harina
- 2 tablespoons/8.5 g nonfat dried milk powder
- 2 teaspoons/6 g xanthan gum
- ½ teaspoon/3 g fine salt
- 2 large eggs, at room temperature
- 3 tablespoons/42 g unsalted butter, melted and cooled
- Cornmeal, for dusting
- Vegetable oil, for the griddle

Combine the chia seeds, yeast, honey, and warm buttermilk in the bowl of a stand mixer fitted with the paddle attachment and mix well. Set aside for about 10 minutes while the yeast proofs. Combine the millet flour, cornstarch, tapioca flour, sorghum

(recipe continues)

flour, brown rice flour, masa harina, milk powder, xanthan gum, and salt in a deep mixing bowl and whisk well.

When the yeast looks frothy add the eggs and melted butter and mix well. Add the dry ingredients and beat at medium speed until combined. Increase the speed to high and beat the dough for 3 to 5 minutes, or until the dough has the consistency of a thick cake batter that would require spreading in a cake pan; it is too thick to pour.

Lightly grease the inside of a large mixing bowl with vegetable oil or softened butter. Scrape the dough out of the mixer bowl and into the greased bowl, smoothing the top with moistened fingers or a rubber spatula dipped in water. Cover the bowl loosely with a sheet of oiled plastic wrap or a damp tea towel and place it in a warm, draft-free spot. Allow the dough to rise for 1¼ to 1½ hours, or until it has doubled in bulk.

While the dough rises grease eight 3-inch/6 cm egg rings and dust them with brown rice flour. Cover a baking sheet with parchment paper or a silicone baking mat and sprinkle it with cornmeal. Arrange the egg rings on the baking sheet. Punch down the dough. Form the dough into 8 equal balls and insert them into the egg rings. Press the dough in evenly with your hand, leveling the top. Cover the baking sheet with a sheet of oiled plastic wrap and allow it to rise in a warm place for 30 minutes, or until the muffins are puffy.

Preheat the oven to 350°F/175°C. Lightly grease a flat griddle or large skillet and heat it over medium heat.

Transfer 4 of the egg rings to the griddle, using a greased spatula. Cover the egg rings with a pot cover or baking sheet and cook the muffins for 5 minutes. Carefully flip the egg rings with a spatula and tongs and cook the second sides of the muffins for an additional 5 to 7 minutes, or until the bottom is browned. Transfer the cooked

(recipe continues)

muffins to a baking sheet lined with parchment paper or a silicone baking mat and carefully remove the rings. Repeat by cooking the remaining 4 muffins.

Bake the muffins for 10 to 12 minutes, or until they sound hollow when tapped on top. Remove the muffins from the oven and allow them to cool for 30 minutes. Then split them open gently with a fork or slice them.

NOTE:

The muffins are best the day they are baked, but they can be stored refrigerated, tightly covered with plastic wrap, for up to 2 days.

Like many American forms of baked goods, English muffins are a very close cousin of an English baked good; this time it's the English crumpet. They were first called toaster crumpets when they were invented in 1894 by Samuel Bath Thomas, a British immigrant from Plymouth, England, who had moved to New York twenty years earlier. Hotels adopted Thomas's item quickly, and from there he went into widespread distribution.

Popovers

JUST AS AMERICAN BISCUITS and British scones are related, so are American popovers and British Yorkshire pudding. Both are made from an egg batter and are a light and crunchy air-filled treat. Their name comes from the fact that the air in the batter creates steam that pops the rolls over the top of the pan. You'll find these are even lighter and more delightful than those made with wheat flour. They virtually melt in your mouth and deserve a good slather with softened butter while they're still hot.

MAKES 12 POPOVERS

½ cup/79 g brown rice flour
⅓ cup/57 g potato starch
¼ cup/31 g tapioca flour
½ teaspoon/3 g fine salt
¼ teaspoon/0.75 g xanthan gum
1¼ cups/300 ml whole milk, heated to 90° to 100°F/32° to 38°C
4 large eggs, at room temperature
3 tablespoons/42 g unsalted butter, melted and cooled

Preheat the oven to 400°F/200°C and grease a 12-cup popover pan or muffin pan.

Combine the rice flour, potato starch, tapioca flour, salt, and xanthan gum in a deep mixing bowl. Whisk well.

Combine the milk, eggs, and melted butter in a blender or food processor fitted with the steel blade. Blend until smooth. Add the flour mixture and blend until smooth.

Ladle the batter into the prepared cups, filling each two-thirds full.

(*recipe continues*)

Bake for 25 minutes, without opening the oven door. Lower the oven temperature to 350°F/175°C and bake for an additional 10 minutes, or until the tops are browned. Remove the pan from the oven and allow popovers to cool in the tins for 5 minutes, then serve immediately.

NOTE:

The batter can be made up to 4 hours in advance and kept at room temperature. Blend it again to distribute the ingredients before filling the cups. The popovers must be baked just prior to serving.

VARIATIONS:

- Add 2 tablespoons/4 g of chopped fresh herbs (any combination of rosemary, thyme, sage, and parsley) to the batter.
- Add ½ cup/40 g of freshly grated Parmesan cheese to the batter.

Hamburger Buns

THE COMMERCIAL GLUTEN-FREE hamburger buns on the market today are really disappointing. Here you have this totally luscious juicy burger cooked just the way you like it with all your favorite trimmings, and the bun crumbles in your hands. Fret not. Here's the answer to your problem, and I bet you will "fire up the barbie" many times after you make these chewy buns.

MAKES 6 BUNS

2 tablespoons/30 g ground chia seeds
2¼ teaspoons/7 g active dry yeast
1 tablespoon/13 g granulated sugar
1 cup/237 ml whole milk, heated to 110° to 115°F/43° to 46°C
¾ cup/90 g millet flour
½ cup/64 g sorghum flour
⅓ cup/42 g tapioca flour
⅓ cup/43 g cornstarch
2 tablespoons/8.5 g nonfat dried milk powder
1 teaspoon/9 g xanthan gum
1 teaspoon/2 g unflavored gelatin or agar powder
½ teaspoon/3 g fine salt
3 large eggs, at room temperature, divided
4 tablespoons (½ stick)/56 g unsalted butter, melted and cooled
3 tablespoons/24 g sesame seeds or poppy seeds

Combine the chia seeds, yeast, sugar, and warm milk in the bowl of a stand mixer fitted with the paddle attachment and mix well. Set aside for about 10 minutes while the yeast proofs. Combine the millet flour, sorghum flour, tapioca flour, cornstarch, milk powder, xanthan gum, gelatin, and salt in a deep mixing bowl and whisk well.

When the yeast looks frothy add 2 of the eggs and the melted butter and mix well. Add the dry ingredients and beat at medium speed until combined. Increase the speed to high and beat the dough for 3 to 4 minutes, or until the dough has the consistency of a thick cake batter that would require spreading in a cake pan; it is too thick to pour.

Lightly grease the inside of a large mixing bowl with vegetable oil or softened butter. Scrape the dough out of the mixer bowl and into the greased bowl, smoothing the top with moistened fingers or a rubber spatula dipped in water. Cover the bowl loosely with a sheet of oiled plastic wrap or a damp tea towel and place it in a warm, draft-free spot. Allow the dough to rise for 1 hour, or until it has doubled in bulk.

Grease a muffin-top pan with vegetable oil spray. Punch down the dough and divide it into 6 equal parts. Form each part into a ball and place the balls in the indentations of the prepared pan, flattening the tops of the balls slightly with your hand.

Cover the pan with a sheet of oiled plastic wrap or a damp tea towel. Allow the buns to rise in a warm place for 35 to 40 minutes, or until almost doubled in size. Beat the remaining egg and brush it gently over the top of the buns. Sprinkle the tops with sesame seeds.

Preheat the oven to 375°F/190°C toward the end of the rising time.

Bake for 17 to 20 minutes, or until the buns are golden brown, sound hollow and thump when tapped, and have reached an internal temperature of 190°F/87°C on an instant-read thermometer. Place the pan on a cooling rack and allow the buns to cool for 15 minutes before serving.

NOTE:

The buns are best the day they are baked, but they can be stored refrigerated, tightly covered with plastic wrap, for up to 2 days.

(recipe continues)

VARIATIONS:

- If you want to make hot-dog buns, you'll get 8 from this recipe, and you need a three-loaf French baguette pan. Form the dough into 8 equal parts after the first rising and roll each into a log shape about 2 inches/5 cm wide and 6 inches/15 cm long, arranging 3 in two of the indentations and 2 in the last one. Allow the second rising in the pan, and bake for 15 to 17 minutes.
- Add ½ cup grated sharp Cheddar cheese to the dough.
- Cook 1 medium onion, diced, in 2 tablespoons olive oil over medium-high heat for 10 to 12 minutes, or until browned and beginning to become crisp. Pat the onions on the tops of the buns instead of the sesame seeds before baking them.

Buttermilk Biscuits

HAPPILY, I HAVE FOUND that conventional wheat biscuits bake best with cake flour, which minimizes the total amount of gluten to keep them tender and flaky. Baking them with all gluten-free ingredients creates even lighter and flakier biscuits. While similar to English scones, biscuits are a truly American bread form. The 1828 *Webster's Dictionary* defined them as "a composition of flour and butter, made and baked in private families." Recipes for biscuits are found in every nineteenth-century cookbook, especially those printed for a Southern audience.

MAKES 12 BISCUITS

- 2 tablespoons/30 g ground chia seeds
- 1½ cups/355 ml buttermilk
- 1 cup/158 g white rice flour
- ¾ cup/127.5 g potato starch
- ½ cup/62.5 g tapioca flour
- ¼ cup/32 g cornstarch
- 2 tablespoons/24 g gluten-free baking powder
- 2 tablespoons/25 g granulated sugar
- 1½ teaspoons/13.5 g xanthan gum
- ½ teaspoon/3 g fine salt
- 2 large eggs, beaten lightly
- 8 tablespoons (1 stick)/110 g unsalted butter, melted and cooled
- 1 large egg yolk, beaten lightly
- 2 tablespoons/30 ml whole milk

Preheat the oven to 375°F/190°C. Line a baking sheet with parchment paper or a silicone baking mat. Soak the chia seeds in the buttermilk for 15 minutes in a large mixing bowl.

Combine the rice flour, potato starch, tapioca flour, cornstarch, baking powder, sugar, xanthan gum, and salt in another deep bowl. Whisk well.

(recipe continues)

Add the eggs and melted butter to the buttermilk mixture and whisk until smooth. Add the flour mixture and mix until well incorporated.

On the prepared baking sheet, form the dough by dropping a large spoon into 12 equal mounds about 2½ inches/6.25 cm wide. Combine the egg yolk and milk in a small cup. Brush the top of the biscuits with the egg mixture and level the tops.

Bake the biscuits for 12 to 15 minutes, or until browned. Allow the biscuits to cool for 10 minutes on the baking sheet, and then serve immediately.

NOTE:

The biscuits can be made up to 1 day in advance and kept refrigerated, tightly covered with plastic wrap. Reheat them, covered with foil, in a 300°F/150°C oven for 5 to 7 minutes.

VARIATIONS:

- Add ¼ cup/60 g of canned, drained, and chopped mild green chiles and ½ cup/56 g of grated Monterey Jack or jalapeño Jack cheese to the dough.
- Add 2 tablespoons of chopped fresh herbs to the dough.
- Add ½ cup/40 g of freshly grated Parmesan cheese and 1 teaspoon/2 g of Italian seasoning to the dough.
- Add ½ cup/50 g of chopped scallions (white parts and 4 inches of green tops) to the dough.

If you don't use buttermilk very often, it's a waste of money to buy a quart to use less than half in a recipe. Instead, buy buttermilk powder. It's shelved with the baking ingredients in the supermarket. Refrigerate it once opened.

Traditional English Dried Currant Scones

RICH SCONES dotted with zesty dried currants are part of all proper English teas, served with clotted cream and fruit preserves. They are basically a first cousin of the Buttermilk Biscuit (see page 223), and they're wonderful at brunch earlier in the day, too.

MAKES 12 SCONES

½ cup/118 ml freshly squeezed orange juice
½ cup/72 g dried currants
1 cup/158 g white rice flour
⅔ cup/113 g potato starch
⅔ cup/83 g tapioca flour
¼ cup/50 g granulated sugar
1 tablespoon/12 g gluten-free baking powder
½ teaspoon/1.5 g xanthan gum
½ teaspoon/3 g fine salt
2 large eggs, at room temperature
¾ cup/178 ml heavy whipping cream, at room temperature
¼ cup/59 ml sour cream, at room temperature
1 large egg yolk, beaten lightly
2 tablespoons/30 ml whole milk

Preheat the oven to 400°F/200°C. Line a baking sheet with parchment paper or a silicone baking mat. Bring the orange juice to a boil in a small saucepan or microwave-safe bowl. Add the currants and allow them to soak for 15 minutes, or until needed.

Combine the rice flour, potato starch, tapioca flour, sugar, baking powder, xanthan gum, and salt in a deep mixing bowl. Whisk well.

(recipe continues)

Combine the eggs, cream, and sour cream in another mixing bowl and whisk until smooth. Drain the currants, discarding any leftover orange juice, and add them to the wet ingredients. Add the flour mixture to the wet ingredients and whisk well.

On the prepared baking sheet, form the dough by dropping a large spoonful of dough into 12 equal mounds about 1½ inches/3.75cm high. Combine the egg yolk and milk in a small cup and mix well. Brush the tops of the scones with the egg mixture and level the tops.

Bake the scones in the middle of the oven for 14 to 17 minutes, rotating the baking sheet after 8 minutes, or until they are browned and a toothpick inserted in the center comes out clean. Allow the scones to cool for 10 minutes on the baking sheet, and then serve immediately.

NOTE:

The scones can be made up to 1 day in advance and kept refrigerated, tightly covered with plastic wrap. Reheat them, covered with foil, in a 300°F/150°C oven for 5 to 7 minutes.

VARIATIONS:

- Substitute dried cranberries or finely chopped dried apricots for the dried currants in the dough.
- Add 1 tablespoon/6 g of grated orange zest and 1 teaspoon/2 g of grated lemon zest to the dough.
- Substitute firmly packed dark brown sugar for the granulated sugar.

It sounds very fancy to say you're serving clotted cream with your scones as part of a tea, but it's really easy to make yourself and far less expensive than the commercial clotted creams on the market. Whisk 4 ounces/113 g of mascarpone with 1 cup/237 ml of heavy whipping cream in a bowl and allow it to sit at room temperature for 15 minutes. If you like, add 2 tablespoons/25 g of granulated sugar and ¼ teaspoon/1.2 ml of pure vanilla extract to the mixture.

Cheddar Rolls

THESE LIGHT AND AIRY ROLLS are a variation of *pão de queijo*, cheese rolls served in Brazil. The exterior is crispy while the interior is soft and eggy, similar to a cream puff.

MAKES 18 ROLLS

8 tablespoons (1 stick)/110 g unsalted butter, sliced
½ cup/118 ml whole milk
1 tablespoon/15 ml Dijon mustard
½ teaspoon/3 g fine salt
2 cups/250 g tapioca flour
2 large eggs
⅔ cup/75 g grated sharp Cheddar cheese
Freshly ground black pepper as desired

Preheat the oven to 375°F/190°C and line 2 baking sheets with parchment paper or silicone baking mats.

Combine the butter, milk, mustard, and salt in a small saucepan and bring to a boil over medium-high heat, stirring occasionally. Remove the pan from the heat and add the tapioca flour all at once. Beat until smooth, using a wooden paddle or wide wooden spoon. Place the saucepan over high heat and beat the mixture constantly for 1 to 2 minutes, or until it forms a mass that pulls away from the sides of the pan and begins to form a film on the bottom of the pot.

Transfer the mixture to a food processor fitted with the steel blade. Add the eggs, one at a time, beating well between each addition and scraping the sides of the work bowl between each addition. Then add the cheese and pepper and mix well again.

(recipe continues)

Using a soup spoon dipped in cold water, form the dough into 2-tablespoon/30 ml mounds on the baking sheets, allowing 2 inches/5 cm between the puffs. Bake the rolls for 18 to 20 minutes, or until lightly browned. Allow the rolls to cool for 10 minutes on the baking sheet, then serve immediately.

NOTE:

The rolls can be prepared up to 6 hours in advance and kept at room temperature. Reheat the rolls in a microwave oven. Microwave on HIGH (100 percent power) in 20-second intervals until hot.

VARIATIONS:

- Substitute freshly grated Parmesan, Romano, or Asiago cheese for the Cheddar.
- Add ¼ cup/28 g of finely chopped cooked bacon or ham to the dough.
- Add 3 tablespoons/20 g of finely chopped sun-dried tomatoes to the dough.

Maple Sweet Potato Rolls

THESE VIVIDLY COLORED DENSE and chewy rolls are slightly sweet, and they are a great brunch bread served with butter or creamed cheese, as well as an accompaniment to any simple roasted poultry or pork at dinner. If you have any left over, use them for bread pudding, adding some raisins and toasted nuts to the egg mixture.

MAKES 12 ROLLS

1½ pounds/680 g sweet potatoes or yams
⅓ cup/40 g millet flour
⅓ cup/42 g sorghum flour
¼ cup/31 g tapioca flour
¼ cup/32 g cornstarch
¼ cup/42.5 g potato starch
3 tablespoons/12.75 g nonfat dried milk powder
1 tablespoon/12 g gluten-free baking powder
1 teaspoon/9 g xanthan gum
½ teaspoon/2 g baking soda
½ teaspoon/1 g ground cinnamon
½ teaspoon/3 g fine salt
Pinch of freshly grated nutmeg
8 tablespoons (1 stick)/110 g unsalted butter, cut into ½-inch/1.25 cm cubes
½ cup/118 ml buttermilk, shaken
⅓ cup/79 ml pure maple syrup

Preheat the oven to 400°F/200°C and line a baking sheet with heavy-duty aluminum foil. Scrub the potatoes and prick them with the tines of a fork. Bake the sweet potatoes, turning them midway through, for 40 minutes, or until the flesh is very tender when pierced with a paring knife. Remove the sweet potatoes from the oven and cut them in half lengthwise. When cool enough to handle, scrape out and mash the pulp. You should have 1 cup/225 g.

(recipe continues)

Increase the oven temperature to 425°F/215°C and grease a standard 12-cup muffin tin.

Combine the millet flour, sorghum flour, tapioca flour, cornstarch, potato starch, milk powder, baking powder, xanthan gum, baking soda, cinnamon, salt, and nutmeg in a food processor fitted with the steel blade. Process, using on-and-off pulsing, until well mixed.

Add the butter to the processor and pulse until the mixture resembles coarse meal. Add the sweet potato, buttermilk, and syrup and process until well combined.

Scoop the dough into the prepared pan, smoothing the tops with a rubber spatula dipped in water. Bake the rolls for 20 to 22 minutes, or until a toothpick inserted in the center comes out clean. Check the rolls after they have baked for 15 minutes and cover them loosely with foil if they are getting too brown.

Place the pan on a cooling rack and allow the rolls to cool for 15 minutes before serving.

NOTE:

The rolls are best the day they are baked, but they can be stored refrigerated, tightly covered with plastic wrap, for up to 2 days.

VARIATIONS:

- Add ¾ cup/87 g of chopped walnuts, toasted in a 350°F/175°C oven for 5 to 7 minutes or until browned, to the dough.
- Add ½ cup/72 g of dried currants or finely chopped dried apricots to the dough.

When you're poking any baked good with a toothpick to judge if it's done, the toothpick has to be made from wood and not plastic. Wood holds wet crumbs, whereas plastic does not. Another way to test is with a strand of dry spaghetti. It, too, holds wet crumbs.

Maple Walnut Breakfast Rolls

I'VE NEVER MET A PERSON who couldn't be lured out of bed by the aroma of buttery sweet rolls baking in the oven. These are crowned with crispy toasted walnuts, and the sweetness comes from maple sugar, another famous New England specialty.

MAKES 12 ROLLS

DOUGH

2¼ teaspoons/7 g active dry yeast

1 cup/237 ml honey, divided

1 cup/237 ml whole milk, heated to 110° to 115°F/43° to 46°C

½ cup/79 g brown rice flour, plus more if needed

½ cup/62.5 g tapioca flour

2 cups/256 g cornstarch

1 tablespoon/9 g xanthan gum

½ teaspoon/3 g fine salt

2 large eggs, at room temperature

8 tablespoons (1 stick)/110 g unsalted butter, melted and cooled

1 teaspoon/5 ml pure vanilla extract

GLAZE AND FILLING

2 cups/234 g chopped walnuts, divided

6 tablespoons (¾ stick)/85 g unsalted butter, melted, divided

1¼ cups/300 ml maple sugar, divided

¼ cup/59 ml light corn syrup

2 tablespoons/30 ml heavy whipping cream

¼ teaspoon/½ g freshly grated nutmeg

¼ teaspoon/0.5 g ground ginger

Combine the yeast, 2 tablespoons/30 ml of the honey, and ¼ cup/59 ml of the warm milk in the bowl of a stand mixer fitted with the paddle attachment and mix well. Set aside for about 10 minutes while the yeast proofs. Combine the ½ cup/79 g of rice flour

(recipe continues)

and the tapioca flour, cornstarch, xanthan gum, and salt in a deep mixing bowl and whisk well.

When the yeast looks frothy add the remaining ¾ cup/178 ml of warm milk, the remaining ⅞ cup/207 ml of honey, and the eggs, melted butter, and vanilla and mix well. Add the dry ingredients and beat at medium speed until combined. Increase the speed to high and beat the dough for 3 to 5 minutes, or until the dough has the consistency of a drop biscuit dough. Add additional rice flour by 1-tablespoon/15 ml/10 g amounts, if necessary.

Lightly grease the inside of a large mixing bowl with vegetable oil or softened butter. Scrape the dough out of the mixer bowl and into the greased bowl, smoothing the top with moistened fingers or a rubber spatula dipped in water. Cover the bowl loosely with a sheet of oiled plastic wrap or a damp tea towel and place it in a warm spot. Allow the dough to rise for 1 hour, or until it has doubled in bulk.

While the dough rises, make the glaze and filling. Preheat the oven to 350°F/175°C. Toast the walnuts on a baking sheet for 5 to 7 minutes, or until browned.

Combine 5 tablespoons/71 g of the melted butter, 1 cup/201 g of the maple sugar, the corn syrup, and cream in a small saucepan. Bring to a boil over medium heat, stirring occasionally. Grease a 13 × 9-inch/33 × 23 cm baking pan with vegetable oil spray. Pour in the glaze and sprinkle the toasted nuts on top of it.

For the filling, combine the remaining tablespoon/14 g of melted butter, the remaining maple sugar, the nutmeg, and ginger in a mixing bowl. Set aside.

Grease your hands with vegetable oil spray. Punch down the dough and divide it into 12 equal portions. Place some of the filling in the center of each piece of dough and arrange the buns in the prepared pan.

Cover the pans lightly with a sheet of oiled plastic wrap or a tea towel and allow them to rise for 1 hour, or until very puffy.

Preheat the oven to 350°F/175°C toward the end of the rising time.

Bake the rolls for 30 to 35 minutes, or until brown. Remove the pan from the oven, allow the buns to cool for 10 minutes, then invert the buns onto a platter. Scrape any glaze remaining in the pan on top of the buns, and serve warm.

NOTE:

While best right out of the oven, the buns can be baked up to 2 days in advance and kept at room temperature, tightly covered. Reheat them, covered with foil, in a 300°F/150°C oven for 8 to 10 minutes.

VARIATIONS:

- Substitute firmly packed light brown sugar for the maple sugar, and substitute pecans for the walnuts. Add 2 teaspoons/5 g of ground cinnamon to the filling.
- Add 1 cup/145 g of raisins to the filling.

Honey, a miraculous substance generated by bees and flowers, has more sweetness than refined sugar, and it is also loaded with nutrients instead of the empty calories of granulated sugar. Honey has been used over the centuries to salve wounds, and studies have shown that it can lower cholesterol. The subtle flavor nuances of honey change depending on the particular flower the bees were working on, and, in general, raw honey is a better choice than processed honey because it contains far more nutrients.

Index

Note: Page references in *italics* indicate recipe photographs.

C

T

V